CINÉ-FILES: The French Film Guides
Series Editor: Ginette Vincendeau

From the pioneering days of the Lumière brothers' Cinématographe in 1895, France has been home to perhaps the most consistently vibrant film culture in the world, producing world-class directors and stars, and a stream of remarkable movies, from popular genre films to cult avant-garde works. Many of these have found a devoted audience outside France, and the arrival of DVD is now enabling a whole new generation to have access to contemporary titles as well as the great classics of the past.

The Ciné-Files French Film Guides build on this welcome new access, offering authoritative and entertaining guides to some of the most significant titles, from the silent era to the early twenty-first century. Written by experts in French cinema, the books combine extensive research with the author's distinctive, sometimes provocative perspective on each film. The series will thus build up an essential collection on great French classics, enabling students, teachers and lovers of French cinema both to learn more about their favourite films and make new discoveries in one of the world's richest bodies of cinematic work.

Ginette Vincendeau

Published Ciné-Files:
*Alphaville* (Jean-Luc Godard, 1965) – Chris Darke
*Amélie* (Jean-Pierre Jeunet, 2001) – Isabelle Vanderschelden
*Casque d'or* (Jacques Becker, 1952) – Sarah Leahy
*Cléo de 5 à 7* (Agnès Varda, 1962) – Valerie Orpen
*La Grande Illusion* (Jean Renoir, 1937) – Martin O'Shaughnessy
*La Haine* (Mathieu Kassovitz, 1995) – Ginette Vincendeau
*La Règle du jeu* (Jean Renoir, 1939) – Keith Reader
*La Reine Margot* (Patrice Chereau, 1994) – Julianne Pidduck
*Le Corbeau* (Henri-Georges Clouzot, 1943) – Judith Mayne
*Les Diaboliques* (Henri-Georges Clouzot, 1955) – Susan Hayward
*Nikita* (Luc Besson, 1990) – Susan Hayward
*Rififi* (Jules Dassin, 1955) – Alastair Phillips
*Un chien andalou* (Luis Buñuel, 1929) – Elza Adamowicz

# Rififi

(Jules Dassin, 1955)

Alastair Phillips

I.B. TAURIS

LONDON · NEW YORK

Published in 2009 by I.B.Tauris & Co. Ltd
6 Salem Road, London W2 4BU
175 Fifth Avenue, New York NY 10010
www.ibtauris.com

Distributed in the United States and Canada Exclusively by Palgrave Macmillan
175 Fifth Avenue, New York NY 10010

ISBN: 978 1 84885 055 2

A full CIP record for this book is available from the British Library
A full CIP record for this book is available from the Library of Congress

Library of Congress catalog: available

Copy-edited and typeset by Oxford Publishing Services, Oxford
Printed and bound in India by Thomson Press India Ltd

# Contents

# Acknowledgements

My research for this project was kindly funded by the Arts and Humanities Research Council (AHRC) and the British Academy. I am very grateful to these two organizations for their generous assistance. I would also like to thank my former workplace, the University of Reading, especially the Department of Film, Theatre & Television, for its nurturing encouragement and support.

I would like to express my gratitude to the following institutions for helping me with access to invaluable materials: in Paris, the Bibliothèque des Littératures Policières, Bibliothèque Nationale and Bifi; in London, the British Film Institute National Film Library and, closer to home in Oxford, the Bodleian Library.

This book owes an enormous debt to its editor, Ginette Vincendeau, whose scholarship has remained such a source of genuine inspiration to me over the years. She has been a wise, supportive and very patient guide.

Thanks too to the following individuals for their various kinds of support and assistance: Jonathan Bignell; Selina Cohen; Ed Gallafent; Peter Graham; Theodora Hadjeandreou; Susan Hayward; Jim Hillier; Frank Krutnik; Mark Kurzemnieks; Valerie Orpen and Lib Taylor.

And, finally, I am pleased to mention the Libros de Cine bookshop in Madrid who supplied my unusual *Rififi* fridge magnet that has been with me as I write. Thankfully, my fridge has been easier to get into than the safe at Mappin & Webb.

Note: Although the title of this book refers to the Anglo-Saxon version, *Rififi*, I have preferred to retain the original French, *Du rififi chez les hommes*, throughout the main body of the text. All other French film titles have been transcribed in this way too. Translations from French to English are by the author except where indicated.

# Plot synopsis

The ageing Parisian gangster, Tony le Stéphanois, has been released from prison and resumes contact with his younger protégé, Jo le Suedois. We learn that Tony, the godfather of Jo's five-year-old son, Tonio, had taken the rap for a failed robbery five years earlier in order to spare Jo's family. He is now a broken man. To redeem Tony's standing in the underworld and to make their fortunes, Jo and Mario Ferrati, a fellow criminal, persuade their mentor to take part in a daring heist from the international jewellers, Mappin & Webb. They recruit a fourth member of the gang: César le Milanais. Meanwhile, Tony discovers that his former lover, Mado, has moved in with Pierre Grutter, the owner of a nightclub in Montmartre called L'Age d'Or. Tony meets up with Mado and beats her. Mado's friend, Viviane, performs a song called 'Rififi' in the club and seduces César.

The meticulously planned robbery goes ahead with the men stealing a cache of jewels by entering the shop from the ceiling of the owner's apartment above the premises. They resolve to stay underground but César cannot resist offering a ring to Viviane. Believing it to be a fake, she shows it to Pierre Grutter and his drug-addicted brother, Rémi. The pair quickly deduce who had been behind the robbery recently announced in the paper. Instead of claiming the reward offered by the Paris police, they resolve to capture the loot themselves.

The Grutters quickly force César to betray his fellow thieves and the pair break into Mario and his girlfriend Ida's apartment where they cut the couple's throats after Ida warns Tony on the phone about what has happened. Tony returns to the deserted L'Age D'Or and avenges these deaths by killing César who has been left bound in the darkness backstage. The Grutters resort to kidnapping Tonio and hold him to ransom. Jo wants to relent to their demands with his share of the money but Tony urges caution.

With the aid of Mado, he traces the villa just outside Paris where Tonio is being held and tricks Rémi's drug supplier into leading the way. At a crucial moment, just as he is about to board the train in pursuit, Tony fails to speak to Jo on the phone to tell him what is happening. Tony reaches the villa, kills Rémi and rescues Tonio just as Jo relents and leaves Paris himself with the laundered cash from the robbery. Tony makes a call from a café and finds out what has happened. Leaving Tonio, he returns to the villa and discovers that Jo has already been murdered on arrival by Pierre Grutter. A shootout ensues and Grutter is also killed. Tony, now injured, manages to return to Paris with Tonio but just as he arrives at Jo's house, he collapses at the wheel of the car. A crowd gathers and a police officer removes the untouched loot from the rear seat.

# Introduction

*Du rififi chez les hommes* (1955) directed by the American émigré film director, Jules Dassin, during his period of politically motivated exile in France during the mid-1950s, is widely acknowledged to be an archetypal French film noir. But when the film was re-released to broad acclaim at the turn of the millennium in France, Britain and the United States, its reputation seemed even to exceed it national origins. The veteran British film critic, Philip French, was typical of many when he argued that Dassin's nail-biting tale of a Parisian gangster heist gone wrong was simply 'one of the greatest crime movies ever made.'[1]

While acknowledging many of the important aesthetic elements that do indeed make up the distinctively French character of *Du rififi chez les hommes*, in this study I shall also examine its specific historical status as an émigré text. Dassin's film raises a number of fascinating questions about the nature of the cultural relations between France and America in the 1950s. In this book I shall thus, in part, focus on the fluid interaction between postwar American and French cinema at a time of contradictory admiration and hostility on the part of the French in the years leading up to the Nouvelle Vague. In particular, we shall see the extent to which the thriller became *the* key site from which to observe the tensions felt by an industry that sought to counter the increasing cultural and economic hegemony of American popular culture with the creative possibility of refracting crime cinema through a distinctively national lens. Using Dassin's version of the Série Noire novel by Auguste Le Breton as a case-study, I want to suggest that *Du rififi chez les hommes* may be seen as an especially fascinating limit-case for understanding these cultural ambivalences. Given that the film was a cinematic adaptation of an American influenced French crime novel, which was then shot in France by an émigré American director, the film raises the interesting possibility of a challenge to normative fixed defintions of cultural identity and national cinema at a time when both film critics and political and cultural analysts perhaps sought to repress such concerns.

This French Film Guide provides a detailed history of *Du rififi chez les hommes*' production, representational and reception contexts, and as such, it raises a series of intersecting subsidiary questions. To what extent did Dassin's status as an American émigré inform the production history of the film, particularly considering the political dimension of his career as a film noir director forced to leave the USA because of the investigations of the House Un-American Activities Committee (HUAC)? How can Dassin's film be situated in relation to the concurrent resurgence of the thriller in French popular culture, especially in terms of the work of the crime novelist Auguste Le Breton and the release of Jacques Becker's seminar gangster film, *Touchez pas au grisbi*, the preceding year? Did *Du rififi chez les hommes* in any way blur the specifically national components within crime drama of the period in terms of its narrative construction, employment of *mise-en-scène* and reference to French performance style and representation of place? How was the film received within the French press in relation to its status as a French crime film, as an adaptation of a best-selling novel and in terms of its contribution to the evolution of a genre now distinguished by shifts in the representation of screen violence and sexuality? Were these concerns marked by the political affiliations of the press and critics and, if so, did they become subsumed into a broader rhetoric about the dialectical nature of Franco-American cultural relations?

In Chapter 2 I concentrate on the events leading up to the production of *Du rififi chez les hommes* by providing a narrative account of the significance to the film of Dassin's career to date. I examine how Dassin's politics and ethics as a filmmaker mattered both to his role as a director of several important American film noirs and to the ways in which the French, in turn, then viewed him as a key figure in the development of this major postwar genre. In that chapter I also provide a history of French film noir and the crucial role that the development of the Série Noire played in revitalizing French crime cinema of the 1950s. I conclude with a detailed survey of the film's production history by paying especial attention to the ways in which Dassin's fellow contributors such as Philippe Agostini,

Alexandre Trauner and Georges Auric made a formative contribution to the look, sound and feel of the text.

In Chapter 3 I provide a detailed interpretative analysis of the important aspects of the film's narrative and *mise-en-scène*. I cover the innovative ways in which Dassin and his collaborators established what would subsequently be seen as a blueprint for the heist film. I also pay close attention to the ways in which the film interprets the two key generic spaces of the nightclub and the city in order to explore broader issues concerning gender, ethics and morality. The purpose of this is also to establish the basis for a subsequent discussion of whether or not the film may, in fact, be legitimately seen as a transnational film noir.

These issues are taken up further in Chapter 4, which broadly concerns the various ways in which the French (and international) press received *Du rififi chez les hommes* in the aftermath of its stunning success at the Cannes Film Festival. I argue that the film became a fascinating touchstone for a set of important critical debates about the nature of cinematic realism and suggest that Dassin's film, because of its distinctive production history and aesthetics, provides a unique vantage point from which to observe broader French film industry trends of the time.

Finally, in Chapter 5, we have the chance to explore the legacy of *Du rififi chez les hommes* and see how, right up to the present day, the term 'Rififi' has become a byword for criminal glamour and the pleasure of engaging with the lasting international dimensions of a true classic of French popular genre cinema.

### Note

1.  Philip French, *The Observer*, 18 August 2002, page unknown.

# 1    The Route to *Rififi*

## A cosmopolitan life

Jules Dassin (1911–2008) was born with a French-sounding name in Middletown, Connecticut in the United States. This intersection between Europe and the New World haunted his career, perhaps at no time more than when he was working on the film that is the subject of this book. Despite the peaceful sobriety of the name 'Middletown' – a location that because of its apparent indeterminacy might also describe Dassin's subsequent life history as well the democratic aspirations of its forebears – the boy's parents moved to New York where their son was raised in Harlem and educated in the Bronx. Dassin's parents were Russian by origin (they were born in Odessa) and their decision to raise Jules in what was then the most cosmopolitan city in the world had an indelible impact on his subsequent worldview. In the mid-1930s, Dassin travelled throughout Europe, especially to countries that would later provide temporary and permanent homes to him in his professional life: France, Greece and Italy. On return, he found employment in New York's Yiddish theatre and worked for the famous Artef Theater on 247 West 48th Street in Manhattan.[1] As a measure of his enduring chameleon-like qualities, he learned Yiddish especially in order to converse with his fellow theatre workers.

The cultural milieu in which Dassin thrived during this period provided a formative influence on his later political and cultural sensibilities. It was during this time that he was exposed to New York's vital left-wing theatre then flourishing in the progressive climate of the New Deal. Dassin would later claim, for example, that he joined the Communist Party after seeing the Group Theatre production of Clifford Odets's episodic drama, *Waiting for Lefty*, set among a community of taxi drivers on the verge of a strike during the Great Depression of the 1920s. Like Orson Welles, Dassin also worked in radio and it was his audio adaptation of Gogol's *The Overcoat* that led to him being noticed by the Broadway producer, Martin Gabel, who subsequently invited him to direct *The Medicine Show* by Oscar Saul and H. R. Hays at the New Yorker Theater. This, in turn, led to an invitation to work in Hollywood.

## Hollywood and film noir

The historical crucible of New York's immigrant culture, radical politics and thriving theatre networks into which Dassin tapped, inspired the spread of liberal democratic ideas when many of its luminaries moved to the Hollywood studio system in Los Angeles.[2] Dassin initially went to the West Coast with two of his colleagues from Artef, Benno Schneider and David Opatoshu, and was employed by RKO for six months where he worked on the sets of *They Knew What They Wanted* (Garson Kanin, 1940) and Alfred Hitchcock's *Mr and Mrs Smith* (1941). He was then hired on a generous seven-year contract by MGM where an early short film he directed, *The Tell-Tale Heart* (1941), based on an Edgar Allan Poe short story, won an Academy Award. This led to his first feature, *Nazi Agent* (1942), which starred the German émigré actor Conrad Veidt. Dassin's subsequent film, *Reunion in France* (1942), is of historical interest in the light of *Du rififi chez les hommes*, his first 'true' French film 14 years later. It was a wartime resistance drama, also set in France and improbably starred Joan Crawford (opposite John Wayne) as a patriotic French aristocrat, Michele de la Becque. It was an enormous commercial success.

Perhaps because of his experiences in New York, Dassin eventually became dissatisfied with the conservative regime at MGM and, after his contract expired in 1947, he signed up with the liberal crime journalist Mark Hellinger's newly formed production unit that had recently been contracted to Universal.[3] Hellinger's influence was timely. He had already produced the émigré director Robert Siodmak's influential film noir, *The Killers*, the previous year and was attuned to the new postwar climate that favoured a greater degree of social realism within the Hollywood crime film. Like the producer Louis de Rochemont, whose works for Fox such as Henry Hathaway's *House on 92nd Street* (1945) and Elia Kazan's *Boomerang!* (1947) Dassin keenly admired, Hellinger wanted a wider use of location cinematography and a greater degree of psychological intimacy shown towards the motivations of his central protagonists. In short, he foresaw a visual equivalence between the drama of the front cover photo of a city newspaper and the true-to-life sensation of a film set on the streets where such a paper would be sold.

Dassin's first film for Hellinger was *Brute Force* (1947), a prison drama whose powerful and intimate examination of male confinement, loyalty and betrayal echoes some of the subsequent concerns of *Du rififi chez les hommes*. Like the film that followed it, *The Naked City* (1948), it avoided the presence of any prominent stars in order to reflect a more democratic concern for the potential of the ordinary human face *in situ*. *The Naked City* was based on the eponymous anthology by the New York photographer Weegee, *Naked City*, which had been published in 1945 to great acclaim. From its opening atmospheric moments, which survey the skyline of Dassin's former home, the film insists on its prominent use of urban location cinematography as a key aspect of the narration. *The Naked City*'s description of city space conveys the vernacular as much as the monumental and the intimate as much as the anonymous, and it attempts to read both these tensions in terms of class. The city is 'naked' because its surface glamour and prestige have been peeled away in favour of a more cautious scrutiny of the way social and economic conditions force people to act the way they do. Like *Du rififi chez les hommes*, it contrasts domesticity with criminality and represents images of play and childhood to suggest another kind of innocence untouched by adult corruption in a dangerous world. The film's scriptwriter Albert Maltz, then already suspected of communist sympathies, attempted to confront the inequities in wealth and status he saw in New York more overtly, but to his and Dassin's bitter regret, Universal clumsily re-edited the film prior to its release.[4]

This did not matter so much to the film's many admirers in France when it was released on 13 May 1949 under the title *La cité sans voiles*.

Writing in the communist newspaper, *Combat,* Jean-Pierre Vivet wrote, for example, that *The Naked City* 'marked an important moment in the development of American cinema ... whose roots lie in the recent school of Italian realism'.⁵ It is interesting to see here how Vivet sees this precursor of *Du rififi chez les hommes* in similar terms as a hybrid 'Euro-American' text. André Bazin likewise observed that while many other American films had been set in New York, 'no film before [*The Naked City*] had revealed such material and human diversity in its portrayal of the poverty, luxury and degradation found in neighbourhoods as varied as those found in Paris'.⁶ Such approving remarks were to form a crucial plank in the way French film culture would subsequently come to view Dassin as 'an outsider within'.⁷

After the early death of Hellinger and a brief return to the New York theatre, the director of *Du rififi chez les hommes* signed with Twentieth Century-Fox and worked with the Armenian émigré author and script-writer, A. I. Bezzerides, on a powerful adaptation of his novel *Thieves' Market, Thieves' Highway* (1949). Bezzerides would go on to have impeccable noir credentials. He had already written the script for Raoul Walsh's atmospheric trucking melodrama, *They Drive By Night* (1940) and would later work on the classic film noirs, *On Dangerous Ground* (Nicholas Ray, 1952) and *Kiss Me Deadly* (Robert Aldrich, 1955). Bezzerides and Dassin's interest in the themes of cooperation, loyalty and betrayal within the milieu of the Californian road haulage industry also bears similarities to *Du rififi chez les hommes.* Both films are driven by a keen eye for the interrelationship between the external immediacies of place and the internal psychological pressures of their troubled masculine protagonists that inhabit these locations.

By the time he had finished the film in January 1949, Dassin was well aware that there were concerns about his future prospects in Hollywood because of the ongoing influence of the House Un-American Activities Committee (HUAC). The HUAC had sought to prove that the American film industry had come under undue influence from the alleged infiltration of Communist Party members or sympathizers. Set up in 1947, it had called the famous 'Hollywood Ten' to the stand the same year; they all cited the Fifth Amendment and refused to testify.⁸ With the publication of a statement by Hollywood's leading executives following these hearings, an enduring informal blacklist had been created, which meant subterfuge on the part of Daryl F. Zanuck in devising something to alleviate Dassin's situation.[9] After the details of one project were leaked to the trade press, incurring the wrath of studio president Spyros P. Skouras,[10] on commencing work on an adaptation of Gerald Kersh's book, *Night and the City*, Zanuck explicitly advised the director that while shooting on location in the UK he should shoot the most expensive sequences first. This was supposedly to circumvent the possibility of him being subsequently fired from the film.[11]

*Night and the City* (1950) is Dassin's intermediary film noir. Made with the American actor Richard Widmark who had had previous roles in Fox urban noirs such as *Kiss of Death* (Henry Hathaway, 1947) and *The Street With No Name* (William Keighley, 1948), the film provides a dramatic portrait of the postwar London underworld. Its transnational status is signalled both by the hybridity of accents – apart from Widmark the film also features the American Gene Tierney and the British Googie Withers – and by the prominence of night-time location signage. In one telling transition, Dassin's even cuts from a view of the illuminated front of the 'American Bar' to the entrance of the 'Café de l'Europe'. The film itself was similarly divided into two in that separate versions were cut for British and American audiences. By the time Dassin returned to Hollywood from Europe, his worst fears had been realized: he was not even allowed onto the Fox lot. His American film career was apparently over.

## The politics of exile

During 1950–51, Dassin returned to Europe and attempted to continue to forge a career in European film production. Ironically, given his own conflicted situation, he worked on preparations for an adaptation of Giovanni Guareschi's best-selling satirical novel, *Le Petit monde de Don Camillo*, starring the beloved French comic actor, Fernandel, as the hot-headed priest constantly at odds with the communist mayor of his village. The film's producer, Guiseppe Amato, who had also produced the neo-realist classic, *Ladri di biciclette/Bicycle Thieves* (Vittorio De Sica, 1948), eventually backed away after concerns that Dassin's presence on the production would damage the prospects of the film obtaining an important American release.[12] While at the Cannes Film Festival in 1951,

Dassin learnt that Frank Tuttle along with Edward Dmytryk had testified against him at the HUAC hearings.[13] He decided to return again to the United States.

There was no work for Dassin in Los Angeles and instead he took up an offer to direct Bette Davies in a Broadway revue called *Two's Company*. It was during rehearsals in 1952 that he was finally summoned by the HUAC to testify. Unlike his friend and colleague from his New York theatre days, Elia Kazan, whose own betrayal in front of the HUAC that same year had so angered him, Dassin never actually got to testify. He insisted that the production of *Two's Company* had to go ahead and, after the intervention of the election of President Eisenhower in November, just as he was getting ready to travel to Washington he received a telegram declaring that his hearing had been postponed indefinitely. Dassin has claimed in various interviews that he would have been a willing participant in the HUAC sessions and would have been prepared to defend himself.[14] This may be the logic of hindsight, but there is no doubt that the episode finally put paid to his employment prospects in the United States.

The following years leading up to *Du rififi chez les hommes* were therefore hard ones for the director and they account for the alacrity with which Dassin eventually began working on the film. He travelled back to France to work on *L'Ennemi public no. 1*, with Fernandel again and Zsa Zsa Gabor. Once more, the blacklist intervened. Jacques Bar, the film's producer, contacted Roy Brewer, head of the International Alliance of Theatrical Stage Employees (IATSE), for information on Dassin. Brewer replied via the IATSE's European representative, Irwing Brown, that Dassin was presumed to have communist links and ten days before shooting was due to commence, he contacted Bar directly saying that if Dassin were employed the film would be denied any kind of release in the United States.[15] This degree of censorship outraged the French. Dassin was by then an admired director in France and for this, as well as his probable symbolic political currency, he was nominated an honorary member of the French directors' union as a mark of solidarity. The French film industry formed a support group led by Jacques Becker whose seminal film noir, *Touchez pas au grisbi* (1954), would become a comparative benchmark of quality for many critics after the release of *Du rififi chez les hommes*. 'L'Affaire Dassin', as it then became known, came to nothing though. Its historical significance remains, as we shall see later, in its status as a key instance of the problematic Franco-American cultural relationship in the postwar period.

Dassin spent his time in a village outside Paris maintaining contact with fellow émigrés such as the blacklisted director John Berry. For a while the authorities revoked his passport. Various projects failed to get off the ground, including adaptations of Giovanni Verga's Sicilian literary classic, *Mastro don Gesualdo* and Emmanuel Roblès's novel, *Cela s'appelle l'aurore*.[16] In the end, it was a phone call from his friend, the producer Henri Bérard, that saved the day. Rather than straightforward high culture, would Dassin turn to one of the best-selling Série Noire books? After years of collaboration and friendship with many of the best practitioners of American film noir, Dassin was now to work on one of the finest *French* film noirs ever made.

### The tradition of French film noir

Jules Dassin's *Du rififi chez les hommes* arrived on French screens at a crucial moment in the tangled critical and production history of French film noir. That one of French film noir's greatest successes was, in fact, directed by an American with substantial experience in its Hollywood equivalent is apt in a way, for it points to the fascinating historical intercultural web underpinning the formation of the genre.

It is worth briefly examining French critical investment in the term 'film noir' before turning to the specificities of the form in France and some preliminary aspects of its subsequent relationship to Dassin's film. It is now largely acknowledged that the term 'film noir', while usually taken to refer to a substantial body of work produced by the Hollywood studios during the 1940s and early 1950s, was in fact coined in France during the late 1930s. Charles O'Brien has noticed, for example, that from January 1938 to September 1939 the term began to appear within French critical discourse in relation to such poetic realist films as *Le Quai des brumes* (Marcel Carné, 1937); *Le Puritain* (Jeff Musso, 1937); *La Tradition de minuit* (Roger Richebé, 1939) and *L'Étrange M. Victor* (Jean Grémillon, 1938).[17] Indeed, writing of the émigré Curt Courant's cinematography in *La Bête humaine* (Jean Renoir, 1938), Emile Vuillermoz specifically noted that '*noir* is currently the colour in fashion in our studios'.[18] What is important here is how what was initially an 'essentially affective response'[19] then also became aligned to entrenched political positions taken up by French critics on the right and left. For both the right-wing François Vinneuil and the left-wing Georges Sadoul, for example, noir had its own pejorative aspect that threatened to contravene 'the morality of the national culture'.[20] Certainly, as we shall later see, this conjugation of transgressive potential and national morality was also to matter in relation to the reception of *Du rififi chez les hommes* in postwar France.

If 'film noir' as a critical term was first employed by French critics in relation to French film, it was also first used by French critics in relation to American cinema. In an important pair of articles published in 1946 in response to the renewed presence of Hollywood cinema on French screens after the years of the Occupation (1940–44), Nino Frank and Jean-Pierre Chartier noted the new perverse criminal psychologies visible in films such as *Murder My Sweet, Double Indemnity* (Billy Wilder, 1944) and *Laura* (Otto Preminger, 1944).[21] Chartier felt that while earlier poetic realist films like *Le Quai des brumes* were redeemed by the presence of love – 'at least the mirage of a better world' – 'there is none of that in the films before us now'.[22] Frank, interestingly in relation to the subsequent impact of Dassin's directorial style in *Du rififi chez les hommes*, also observed the crucial impact of 'facial expressions, gestures, utterances' to the films' narrative style, especially in relation to the evident 'primacy of the script, and the fact that a film is first and foremost a sober story well constructed and presented in an original manner'.[23] 'Has Hollywood definitively outclassed Paris?' he tentatively asked.[24]

French critical praise for American noir style, especially to the detriment of much considered evaluation of the significance of French traditions, continued and reached a kind of apogee with the publication of the seminal critical study by Raymond Borde and Etienne Chaumeton, *Panorama du film noir américain*, in the same year as the release of *Du rififi chez les hommes*. Indeed, the original cover of Borde and Chaumeton's book actually featured a distinctive still from Dassin's *Night and the City* – a powerful signal of the veneration in which the French now held the American film noir director. Dassin, like other major American directors such as Nicholas Ray that the French critics of the 1950s favoured, was seen as both an individual agent – an 'auteur' – and as a victim of the Hollywood system. Borde and Chaumeton explicitly noted, for example, how the personal quality of his work on *Brute Force* and *The Naked City* had suffered at the hands of studio heads at the editing stage. Nonetheless, in 1955 they were able to recollect that 'the simultaneous showing in Paris during winter 1951 of Elia Kazan's *Panic in the Streets* (1950), Jules Dassin's *Night and the City* (1950), and John Huston's *The Asphalt Jungle* (1950) [had been] the cinematic event of the season'.[25] In an echo of the narrative concerns of Dassin's next film noir shot in France, they then described how all three films 'thrust aside the glistening folds in which the modern big city garbs itself by night, in order to plunge into the feverish and desolate world of gambling joints, lowlife types, and nightclubs'.[26]

The period between 1954 and 1955 is particularly crucial in the history of French film noir. In the year leading up to the release of Dassin's film and Borde and Chaumeton's book, the success especially of Becker's *Touchez pas au grisbi* with the French public had led to a proliferation of related titles. For Borde and Chaumeton, the 'season has [now] been placed under the aegis of the "noir"'.[27] Even an Italian melodrama, *Processo contra ignoto* (Guido Brignone, 1952), they noted, had had its anonymous title changed on its French release to the then more fashionable, *C'est la faute au grisbi* [*Blame it on the Loot*].

What then did 'French film noir' consist of in their eyes? Borde and Chaumeton discerned three trends at the time. First, there was the 'criminal psychology based on suspense'[28] such as Henri Georges Clouzot's contemporaneous success, *Les Diaboliques* (1955).[29] Second, there was 'the police documentary' typified by another current hit, *Razzia sur la chnouf* (Henri Decoin, 1955), although the origins of its then current revival, they also suggested, lay in earlier films such as *Quai des Orfèvres* (Henri Georges Clouzot, 1947) and *Un flic* (Maurice de Canonge, 1947). Then, finally, they described the 'films about the underworld' of which Becker's and Dassin's films, despite their significant differences, may be said to be the most prominent and most enduring examples.

Borde and Chaumeton also mentioned the popular success of the critically neglected cycle of low-budget, humorous crime action films begun with André Hunebelle's trilogy starring Raymond Rouleau –*Mission* à *Tanger* (1949), *Méfiez-vous des blondes* (1950) and *Massacre en dentelles* (1951) – and continued by Bernard Borderie's début *Les Loups chassent la nuit* (1952). It is clear, although the writers did not say so at the time, that with the subsequent success of the Lemmy Caution comic-thriller series starring the American émigré actor Eddie Constantine, the supposed lines between French and American film culture were beginning to be deliberately crossed for parodic ends. By 1955, the series that Jean Sacha's *Cet homme est dangereux* (1953) had initiated and that had taken off with Bernard Borderie's *La Môme vert-de-gris* (1953) and *Les Femmes s'en balancent* (1954), had also recently spawned other Eddie Constantine vehicles directed by Dassin's fellow Hollywood émigré, John Berry – *Ça va barder* (1954) and *Je suis un sentimental* (1955). John Berry's own links with the tradition of the American crime film went back to the 1930s when he co-wrote *The Public Enemy* (William Wellman, 1931). He had also directed *Casbah* (1948), the second American remake of *Pépé le moko* (Julien Duvivier, 1937). *Du rififi chez les hommes*, as we are beginning to see, therefore inhabited a complex lineage that points both to a turbulent awareness of the success of the American crime film and to the persistence of a French model, with the possibility of a hybrid model somewhere in between.

We shall return to the complexities of Franco-American film relations with particular reference to the reception of *Du rififi chez les hommes* later on, but now I want to unpick the ways in which the historical account provided of French film noir so far seems to have marginalized certain aspects of the phenomenon in France, especially those that have a particular bearing on the importance of Dassin's film. As Ginette Vincendeau has argued, the spectatorial pleasures involved in watching French crime cinema of the period differed significantly from the American model Frank and Chartier described, especially in terms of the useful distinction that can retrospectively be drawn between the *policier*, typified by the Albert Préjean series of Maigret adaptations such as *Cécile est morte* (Maurice Tourneur, 1944), and what Vincendeau terms the 'social noir', exemplified by films such as *Une si jolie petite plage* (Yves Allégret, 1949).[30] While many *policiers*, especially of the immediate postwar period, were 'predominately recast as light comedy',[31] Vincendeau argues, the darkest films such as *Quai des Orfèvres* were actually ones that relied as much on an atmospheric 'French quotidian realism' as 'generic noir features'.[32] Why then did French critics at the time not immediately link the 'sociological and topographical precision' of French 'social noir' to the success of American film noir? In part, it was due to the immediate legacy of the Occupation and a negative association between the legacy of the visual style of poetic realism and the tragedy of defeat. As Vincendeau puts it, 'since the term [had been] generally used in France in a derogatory way, [noir temporarily] needed to be detached from its French context in order to *celebrate* the American films.'[33]

*Du rififi chez les hommes* and *Touchez pas au grisbi* thus suggest a turning point in the generic evolution of French crime cinema. Neither film appears especially marked by any of the pervasive melancholy or despair of poetic realism. As François Guérif has noted, immediately prior to the resurgence of the gangster film in the mid-1950s, narratives favouring ordinary people like the author of detective novels in *Le Témoin de minuit* (Dimitri Kirsanoff, 1953) or the director of a municipal library in *Leur dernière nuit* (Georges Lacombe, 1953) had increasingly come to deglamourize the representation of crime.[34] These were characters affected not so much by tragic pre-destiny as the momentary flash of emotional impulse. *Touchez pas au grisbi* and *Du rififi chez les hommes* present a significant variant of this relationship to the everyday, which in the case of the latter was especially conveyed by its explicit association with criminal literature. The author of its source novel, Auguste Le Breton (1913–99), publicly vaunted his affinity with the real-life underworld of Paris – an association, he argued, directly informed the subject of his story. The audience's relationship to criminal activity was therefore not mediated through the depiction of the act of writing or librarianship, as was the case with the films of Kirsanoff and Lacombe; it was compellingly suggested by the detailed immersion in the experiential act of crime itself.

This attention to location and character detail is what makes French cinema's return to the gangster genre so noteworthy. Although *Touchez pas au grisbi* and *Du rififi chez les hommes* differ in terms of their actual treatment of the heist – all the narrative action in the former takes place after the event – they both offer a familiar topography of nocturnal city streets, bars, restaurants and nightclubs, which provides the setting for the unravelling of familial loyalties centred on the figure of an ageing criminal patriarch (played by Jean Servais and Jean Gabin respectively). The films have a melancholic seasonal air in their Parisian location sequences that further accentuates the intimacy and familiarity of their intricately detailed interiors. This is especially true in the carefully realized portrayal of Madame Bouche's restaurant in *Touchez pas au grisbi*, which serves as a kind of protective maternal space apart from the masculine treachery of the world outside. Vincendeau has argued that the emphasis in these films on the representation of virile masculinity and the themes of 'loyalty and betrayal' enhances the way in which they may be read as coded representations of the Occupation.[35] This is a convincing argument but, as she also points out, it is equally important to note how a sense of transition is also evoked in terms of the films' dramatic structure and the depiction of competing interests signalled by the 'old France' and 'the new'. The tensions within the male groups in both films portray not just a battleground that has echoes of the past, but one that also points to a nation in transition. In *Touchez pas au grisbi* this is exemplified by Max's awareness of both his own ageing process and the generational shift underway within the underworld. It is symptomatic, if also problematic, for example, that at the end of the film he decides to relinquish his French Renault – whose 'F' for France is repeatedly brought to the forefront in the film's *mise-en-scène* – for a smart new American car. He subsequently visits Madame Bouche's restaurant in it, but now sits apart from the others with his new American girlfriend, Betty. In *Du rififi chez les hommes*, the 'changing of the guard' is visible in the contrast between Tony's decrepitude and the strength of Pierre, the boss of the Grutter clan, as well as the relationship between the ailing French gangster and his godson, Tonio, who turns instead to Hollywood for his cultural influence.

## Auguste Le Breton and the Série Noire

The intercultural formation of Jules Dassin's adaptation of Auguste Le Breton's novel was but one further instance of the complex relationship between European and American forms within the associated spheres of French crime literature and French crime cinema. In her study of the influence of the *roman noir* on French postwar culture, Claire Gorrara points out that the publication of the first true French detective novel, Emile Gaboriau's *L'Affaire Lerouge* in 1863, only preceded Charles Baudelaire's translation of the American writer Edgar Allan Poe's short mystery stories such as *Murders in the Rue Morgue* by two years.[36] Similarly, Vincendeau reminds us that the 'dovetailing of French and American traditions in the *policier* genre'[37] within French cinema goes far back to the enormous success with the French public of Victorin-Hippolyte Jasset's *Zigomar* and *Nick Carter* films as well as Louis Feuillade's *Fantômas* serial (1913–14).

The success of the Le Masque collection of crime fiction founded in 1928 and the appearance of Georges Simenon's first Maigret novel, *Pietr le Letton*, in 1931 was paralleled during the 1930s by a proliferation of French translations of American hard-boiled crime novelists such as Dashiell Hammett. Claude-Edmonde Magny has argued that the 'phenomenological' style of this kind of American literature was antithetical to 'the refined French literature of introspection by the likes of [André] Gide and [Marcel] Proust'.[38] This may have been a reason why Gide admired Hammett, but it also accounts for one aspect of the later successful reception of *Du rififi chez les hommes* in France. The film preserved an attention to psychological detail in terms of the representation of local milieux, but in the form of its treatment of the heist, it also sensationally concentrated on the unfurling in real time of an elaborate externally observed physical activity. As Marcel Duhamel, the founder of the Série Noire, would later say, 'as in all good movies, feelings are expressed by gestures'.[39]

The immediate precursor of the Série Noire was the Collection Minuit, which began during the Occupation when the French public was officially denied access to American crime film and fiction. As Gorrara suggests, one of the functions of this particular series ghost-written by French authors (often with American-sounding pseudonyms) was clearly to depict 'an imaginary America in sharp contrast to ration-obsessed wartime France'.[40] This interrelationship between American and French traditions continued with the arrival of the Série Noire in 1948. Indeed, it is interesting to note that the very early books in the later highly successful series were actually translations of works by the English writers Peter Cheyney and James Hadley Chase, who were writing pastiches of American crime fiction precisely because they too had never travelled to the USA!

Marcel Duhamel's simple aim in initiating the Série Noire format was to 'stop [his readers] from falling asleep'.[41] To this end, he came from an appropriate pedigree, thanks to a longstanding association with the Surrealist poet and scriptwriter, Jacques Prévert, who suggested the title of the actual enterprise.[42] Duhamel had also worked in the French cinema during the 1930s. He appeared as an (often unaccredited) actor in numerous films such as *Le Crime de Monsieur Lange* (Jean Renoir, 1936); *Drôle de drame* (Marcel Carné, 1937) and *Carrefour* (Curtis Bernhardt, 1938) and also, appropriately, worked in film dubbing. He had also translated American fiction and it was no surprise therefore that the next tranche of work published in his series consisted of French translations of work by the likes of Raymond Chandler, James M. Cain, Jim Thompson, David L. Goodis, Mickey Spillane and Horace McRoy.[43] This Franco-American cross-cultural fertilization developed further with the subsequent publication of novels by 'Terry Stewart' (the pseudonym of Serge Arcouët), 'John Silver Lee' (Thomas Narcejac) and 'Vernon Sullivan' (Boris Vian).[44] In an interesting reversal of the acculturation process Dassin faced, these writers provided French audiences with the phenomenon of a French writer with an apparently American name writing American-style crime fiction rather than the subsequent phenomenon of an American director with an apparently French name directing French-style crime fiction.

It has been argued that this interest in the Americanization of crime fiction in France may relate to Borde and Chaumeton's previously mentioned dismissal of the legacy of French poetic realism in favour of the critical approval displayed towards the reinvigorated American film noir.[45] But in an interesting twist on this, which has repercussions for the ways in which aspects of Dassin's adaptation of *Du rififi chez les hommes* may be read, Gorrara also suggests that this model of crime literature nonetheless 'offered a privileged narrative for contesting social and political change in France'.[46] Much of the work of this generation of 'American' oriented French writers, she argues, 'focused on controversial and disturbing images of America [in that] they adapted the hard-boiled genre for a transposed critique of their own culture', especially in relation to the influence of American models of capitalism.[47]

If this literature seemingly offered a displayed critique of contemporary France through the refracted lens of an American setting, it was perhaps not surprising then that the Série Noire initially remained a relatively minor taste during these years. Indeed, the series only developed a serious mass appeal with the publication of work by actual French authors such as Albert Simonin and Auguste Le Breton with their seminal novels, *Touchez pas au grisbi* and *Du rififi chez les hommes*.[48] What distinguished these books from their predecessors within the imprint? In two words, it was language and locale. Both titles resonated with a lively and often impenetrable use of gangster slang as if to celebrate the native identity of the criminal protagonists of the narratives. Simonin and Le Breton offered glossaries to their readers at the end of each volume explaining the more abstruse terms used in the dialogue. Each book also offered a return to the centrality of Paris as an enduring mythologized space for criminal, especially gangster, activity. As noted in the case with the subsequent film adaptations, the network of streets, dens, bars and rooms the authors detailed provided an immediately recognizable enveloping community, which then also served as a kind of metonym for the smaller family-like structures of the individual gangs.

Le Breton (born Auguste Montfort in Finistère) was ideally suited to play the role of advocate for this new appeal to cultural authenticity. Both *Du rififi chez les hommes* and *Razzia sur la chnouf* (the screen adaptation of which preceded the former by only one week)[49] were promoted in terms of their author's plausible proximity to the world in which the stories were set. The latter is populated by an extraordinary array of louche, lowlife, Parisian character types, including an immaculately dressed gangland criminal played by Le Breton himself. When the book *Du rififi chez les hommes* was released in January 1954, exactly one year after Simonin's novel, Le Breton claimed that the character of Tony was based on someone he had once known in Montmartre and that other characters resembled people he had known during the Second World War. Later, in two of his semi-fictionalized autobiographies, *Les Hauts murs* and *La Loi des rues*, Le Breton also included photographs of himself in underworld settings and the distinctive quality of these carefully orchestrated images may be likened to stills from a film noir. It clearly suited Le Breton to mythologize himself, but, as Claire Gorrara convincingly suggested, 'more so than almost any other form of popular literature in France, the roman noir [nonetheless offers] the opportunity to re-evaluate French national identity and cultural practice from the bottom up, from the perspective of writers and readers who perceive themselves to be marginal to the literary and political establishment.'[50]

## Production history

Le Breton came to work closely with Dassin on the development of the project, although the American was not apparently the first choice as director once the film's producer, Henri Bérard, optioned the novel. In his autobiography, Le Breton states that he originally had talks with Jean-Pierre Melville and that Yves Campi had also expressed an early interest in the production.[51] According to Jean-Pierre Melville, with whom Le Breton would also later collaborate on the celebrated gangster heist film, *Bob le flambeur* (1955), Melville was actually the person who had persuaded Bérard to purchase the rights to the book in the first place.[52] It is certainly true that his name is mentioned in the existing production file for *Du rififi chez les hommes*,[53] even though there are conflicting accounts about whether Dassin actually knew of Melville's prior involvement before he eventually agreed to take part.[54]

Having said this, Le Breton was later delighted that an American should have directed his second screen adaptation. 'Jules had a degree of international savoir faire,' he commented.[55] He was also pleased that the director had initially envisaged a small role for him again – as a barman – even though this never actually materialized. There was also another possible ulterior motive in inviting a non-Frenchman to proceed with the film. The novel's main villains were North Africans and in the light of the growing unrest in Algeria at the time between the French colonial authorities and the indigenous population, it may have been considered unwise to reproduce this conflict directly within the terrain of the French popular crime film. An American with a proven track record in the genre would offer a different angle. Dassin was reportedly dismayed when he eventually discerned the elements of the project he had been offered. After receiving the tempting call from Henri Bérard, he spoke with a French agent friend of his, Claude Briac, asking him to come over and help him to translate the novel. The book's impenetrable slang was too daunting and the American needed a native hand to help digest the material. When

Dassin discovered the embedded racism of the book's representation of criminality, not to mention the extreme violence of aspects of its narrative, he despaired before eventually relenting, realizing that commercial imperatives had to override ethical concerns.

Dassin worked swiftly on the initial process of adaptation with the veteran scriptwriter, René Wheeler, who had previously written the dialogue for the thriller *Minuit… Quai de Bercy* (Christian Stengel, 1953) as well as having assisted on scripts for more famous films such as Jacques Tati's *Jour de Fête* (1948) and Christian-Jaque's *Fanfan la Tulipe* (1952). He produced a working draft in less than a week, then deferred to Wheeler who helped to retranslate the English language material back into French. Substantial changes were made to the structure of the story in terms of characterization and narrative significance. First, Dassin wanted to recentre the film's emotional core on the cross-generational relationship between the ageing Tony le Stéphanois and his younger protégé, Jo le Suedois. This male pairing would evoke the bond between Max (Jean Gabin) and Riton (René Dary) in the touchstone text of *Touchez pas au grisbi*, the success of which with French filmgoers had helped lead to the decision to film Le Breton's *Razzia sur la chnouf* and *Du rififi chez les hommes*. It preceded the subsequent pairing of Bob (Roger Duchesne) and Paulo (Daniel Cauchy) in *Bob le flambeur*. A decision was also taken to eradicate the North African dimension and concentrate on giving the internecine rivalries within the Parisian underworld a clearer European aspect. This was indicated in the film by the proliferation of different accents (especially the distinctive Italian rhythm of Mario's dialogue) and by the specifically German-sounding name of 'Grutter' that was given to the film's rival gang clan. The presence of the Grutters points back to a restaging of wartime tensions and forward to the future economic competition between France and Germany then coming into view. The latter idea was to be taken up again as a theme in Louis Malle's crime drama, *Ascenseur pour l'échafaud* (1958), just a few years later. Then third, to introduce the ideas of team loyalty and betrayal into the organization of Tony's gang, Dassin decided to instigate the death of the character of César. That Dassin himself played César (under the pseudonym of Perlo Vita[56]) ended up being particularly resonant, for as well as bearing similarities with the treacheries of the Occupation period, the issue very clearly also addressed the director's own predicament as an economic victim of the blacklist betrayed by his former colleagues in Hollywood.

Perhaps the most substantial reworking of the source text was the decision to focus on what had been just a relatively minor element of Le Breton's book – the robbery. This was an enormously prescient idea, for the close attention paid to the minutiae of the heist is what most people remember of the film today and the celebrated nail-biting tension of its realization has led to numerous imitations and homages, not least by Dassin himself when he came to make *Topkapi* (1964) a decade later.[57] At the time though, as Dassin has recalled, the excising of much of Le Breton's novel in favour of the telling of an act of crime and its inevitable unravelling 'was the only way to work my way out of a book that I couldn't do, wouldn't do.'[58] Although Le Breton would later endorse Dassin's restructuring, his immediate response was less positive. Dassin recalls that when the French novelist initially read his script he complained that his book had vanished. 'I tried to explain that's how it is when you adapt a book,' Dassin now says, but 'he took out a gun and plunked it down on the table, and repeated, "Where's my book?" I looked at him, I looked at the gun and I began to laugh. And because I laughed he took me in his arms and we became friends.'[59]

Having resolved their differences, Le Breton immediately took the director under his wing and accompanied Dassin on an improvised tour of lowlife Paris. Dassin remembers how Le Breton (like Bob in *Bob le flambeur*) modelled himself on the gangsters played in the kind of American films he himself had once made. The two even attended the funeral of Pierre Cuc, then known as 'the referee of the French under-world'.[60] Having said this, perhaps because of his natural outsider status as much as his predilection for moral conflict, Dassin never really sought to express a vision of the world of French crime as it really was. What interested him most was character and the focus on the robbery allowed him to delineate with enormous skill individual character psychology as much as the crime itself. He acknowledged this in interview with the French trade press, at the time telling the *La Cinématographie Française*: 'rather than searching to reproduce the ambience of the milieu, I want, above all, to make a film about character and by studying each personality individually I will sometimes by necessity stray from the initial subject [of the drama].'[61]

The casting of *Du rififi chez les hommes* was therefore a vital ingredient in this process. As Lenny Borger points out, Dassin was unable to use a star actor such as Jean Gabin in the lead role of Tony even though Gabin had had a significant role in the success of Becker's *Touchez pas au grisbi*.[62] He would have simply cost too much. The producers therefore turned to the Belgian-born Jean Servais (1910–76) who had had a longstanding career in French cinema in such films as Raymond Bernard's *Les Misérables* (1933) – in which he played Marius – *Angèle* (Marcel Pagnol, 1934); *Jeunesse* (Georges Lacombe, 1934) and *Quartier sans soleil* (Dimitri Kirsanoff, 1939). Servais's career had been in decline because of drinking problems and his postwar persona in such films as *Une si jolie petite plage* (Yves Allégret, 1948) was largely based on a kind of weary, despairing cynicism, which Dassin used to great effect. Central to Servais's performance style was the rich and lived-in timbre of his voice, which had previously lent substance to his role as Maupassant in Max Ophuls's *Le Plaisir* (1952). Several other actors' performances in the film worked in relation to these qualities. First, there was Robert Manuel's (1916–95) vivacious portrayal of the Italian gangster, Mario, whose highly mobile features contrasted vividly with Servais's melancholy reserve. Manuel brought a degree of spirited theatricality to his role, which was unsurprising given his background in the Comédie Française. Manuel too had experience of prewar French cinema – he had appeared in two of G. W. Pabst's émigré films of the period: *Mademoiselle Docteur* (1937) and *Le Drame de Shanghaï* (1939). Second, and very importantly, to strengthen the pan-European aspect of the production, Dassin (apparently on the suggestion of Bérard's wife) cast the relatively unknown Austrian actor, Carl Möhner (1921–2005), in his first French film as Jo le Suedois. Möhner's otherness in terms of both nationality and age brings an awkward tenderness to the interaction between the two leading male characters and it reinforces the hard-bitten vulnerability of Tony who has subsequently become a man out of time. Interestingly, despite the French audience's lack of familiarity with him, Möhner was also the highest-paid actor on the set. He earned 2.1 million francs against Servais who earned 1.8 million.[63] Then finally, there were Marcel Lupovici and Robert Hossein who played the two main members of the Grutter clan. Lupovici was a Romanian born actor whose background helped lend a cosmopolitan edge to his portrayal of the hardened, sleek character of Pierre Grutter. Lupovici had been working in French cinema since the 1930s (like Marcel Duhamel he even had a minor part in *Le Crime de Monsieur Lange*) but his career following *Du rififi chez les hommes* was less successful than that of Robert Hossein who played his brother, Rémi Grutter. Hossein, a French actor whose Russian/Iranian paternal heritage also created an aura of villainous difference to his persona in the film, continued to be cast in crime dramas such as *Brigade antigangs* (Bernard Borderie, 1966). He achieved lasting fame as the romantic lead, Jeoffrey de Peyrac, in the popular series of soft-core *Angélique* films during the 1960s.

Many people remember the film today for its celebrated musical number written by Jacques Larue and Philippe-Gérard and sung by Magali Noël (1932–), which takes place in the L'Age d'Or nightclub. The venue was renamed from the novel's 'Cimeterre d'or' in honour of Luis Buñuel's film of the same name on which the film's production designer, Alexandre Trauner (1906–93), had worked back in the 1920s. Noël, born Magali Noëlle Guiffray in Turkey, had appeared in cabaret since the age of 16 and had only recently made her film début after performing in the French theatre. She had also been cast as Lisette in *Razzia sur la chnouf*. Magali Noël's extraordinarily lithe and sensual performance in the number is undoubtedly one aspect of the way in which the film conforms to the generic convention of having a nightclub song evoke notions of female sexual display and male desire within noir narration, but there is also something excessive about the way she delivers this role. In part, this is due to the need for the song to provide a convincingly over-determined exposition of the meaning of the actual word '*rififi*', which no one in point of fact utters throughout the entire film. But this sense of excess also signals how any sense of the 'female sphere' is rendered unnecessary or 'too much' in the world of men and 'their' troubles. As we shall see later, this pattern of exclusion will be underlined by the film's treatment of women and visual style in a number of other key scenes, including those featuring Mado (Marie Sabouret) and Louise (Janine Darcey). Sabouret hailed from a background in the Comédie Française and had appeared in a number of 1950s costume dramas such as *Si Versailles m'était conté* (Sacha Guitry,

1954) and *Les Trois mousquetaires* (André Hunebelle, 1953). Darcey's film career stretched back to the 1930s when she acted alongside leading talents of the day such as Louis Jouvet in Marc Allégret's *Entrée des artistes* (1938). In 1949, she had a leading role opposite her husband Serge Reggiani in Henri Aisner's adaptation of the popular Gaston Leroux novel, *Le Mystère de la chambre jaune*.

It is worth reinforcing the significance of the film's musical and design aspects. Dassin was certainly fortunate to have been able to work with Alexandre Trauner, the Hungarian émigré set designer best remembered today for his work with Marcel Carné, especially *Les Enfants du paradis* (1945). After the relative failure of Trauner's collaboration with Carné on *Les Portes de la nuit* (1946), he was anxious to redeem himself for his costly and perfectionist reputation within the French production system and took a reduced fee in order to design sets such as the L'Age d'Or and, of course, the bank that was the site of the robbery. The latter was naturally crucial to the film's success, as looking at versions of the film's script reveal.[64] The heist sequence, which will be examined in more detail later on, was densely plotted in advance with a system of fixed shots being closely integrated to form the coherent spatial architecture necessary to the drama. Jean Servais noticed this when recollecting working on the film. 'It seems to me that [the film's] shots were absolutely devised in relation to one another,' he said. 'Preparatory work was thought over very carefully.'[65] Another of the film's prestigious talents, the composer Georges Auric (1899–1983) – whose cosmopolitan career trajectory mirrored that of Dassin's[66] – originally disapproved of Dassin's desire not to score this sequence. According to the director, Auric, whose music dramatically propels the drama forward elsewhere in the film, actually went ahead and scored the sequence to see what it would look and sound like. Dassin invited him to watch the cut film with and without the addition of non-diegetic sound, and he immediately relented.[67]

Perhaps the most important of Dassin's collaborators, and certainly the most underrated, was the cinematographer Philippe Agostini (1910–2001) whose capturing of a wintry Paris and its milky grey light and melancholy hues chimes so carefully with the emotional timbre of the plot.[68] Like many cinematographers of his generation, Agostini – whose Franco-Italian name again signals the cosmopolitan heritage of the film –

had come to professional prominence under the tutelage of the émigré cinematographers of the 1930s. In Agostini's case, he had worked, alongside Trauner, with Curt Courant on *Le Jour se lève* (Marcel Carné, 1939).[69] Like most cinematographers of the classical period in France, Agostini was used to the artificiality of the small-scale studio whose more intimate and evenly modulated lighting aesthetics were largely determined by the economic constraints of the time. Indeed, Vincendeau has argued that this tradition of 'intimate realism' in French cinematic practice had led to one of the distinguishing differences from the more action-oriented American noir model: 'an aesthetics of confinement'.[70] This certainly could not be truer when it comes to a consideration of the heist sequence within *Du rififi chez les hommes*, but the film is also remarkable for its extensive and varied treatment of Parisian topography, which, as the script reveals, was embedded in the construction of the film from its outset. As Dassin told François Truffaut in a production report of the film published in *Arts*, filming on the streets of the French capital did not pose the same number of problems as it had done for him in London and New York.[71] Necessarily, the film displays an interest in class distinctions and the high-class location of the robbery on the Rue de la Paix in contrast with the working-class streets of Belleville and Ménilmontant is but one instance of this. But the film is also interested in a very fluid treatment of city space, as we shall see later, which ranges from the suburbs of St Rémy les Chevreuse through to the Pont de Bir Hakeim and the Place Pigalle. Dassin, in fact, prepared locations very carefully with his secretary and Agostini. He remembers walking everywhere, as a newcomer would, noting the potential of certain streets and vistas. An example of this is the decision to shoot the conclusion of the film within the particular geography of Rue de la Bidassoa in the 20th arrondissement where the distinctive curvature of the streetscape adds a dramatic aspect to the framing and its implications for discerning character relationships. On top of this, the film was very tightly edited by Roger Dwyre, a man who went on to become a regular collaborator on many of Dassin's other European productions. The director remembers the 'daily pleasure' of completing the edit with Dwyre – a process that meant that after years of working within the confines of the Hollywood studio system, he was 'suddenly free' to cut a film as he wished.[72]

In contrast with the detailed precision involved in laying out the shot compositions for the heist sequence, Dassin argued that once a particular location has been decided upon, he preferred a sense of improvisation to take precedence. This was particularly important for the way he worked with his actors – a method no doubt going back to his days in New York theatre. He wanted to see how people looked in relation to each other. Another factor, which played a key role in the time it took for the film to be completed, was the decision he took to avoid shooting in the glare of full sunlight. The team preferred the subdued and atmospheric light of overcast days.[73]

The film's shoot, though taking place on a relatively low final approved budget of 117,517,000 francs, took ten weeks.[74] The cameras started rolling at the Photosonor Studios in Courbevoie on 22 September 1954 and the production was completed on Christmas Day the same year. In total, four weeks and two days were spent in the studio with the rest of the time on location.[75] Dassin was nervous about working again with a crew and a cast after such a long time away from the film industry, and the fact that he was working with an international cast in what was still to him a foreign country exacerbated his initial unease about doing justice to the project. The production files for the film reveal that Société Nouvelle Pathé Cinéma had pitched the idea of filming Le Breton's book with Dassin in charge on the basis, in part, of the novel's success with the French public and Dassin's fame as a director. Records also show that a case was made for the now sustainable popularity of the crime thriller genre with the recent examples of *Touchez pas au grisbi* and *Les Femmes s'en balançent* being cited as models to emulate.[76] This was against a backdrop of reports in the French trade press that by autumn 1954 Jacques Becker's film, released only at the beginning of March, had already taken the phenomenal amount of 129,333,950 francs at the French box-office.[77] Furthermore, there was the sensitive issue of censorship and worries about whether the planned film had eliminated enough of the vicious violence in the source's novel. The pressure was therefore on for Dassin, in particular because of his outsider status, to live up to these commercial concerns.

Just over a week into the shoot, the producers learnt from Henry de Segogne, then president of the Commission de Contrôle des Films Cinématographiques, that the question of the film's representation of criminality and violence had been duly considered. 'Despite considerable unfavourable opinions, the Commission has decided not to oppose the making of this film,' he wrote. 'But it calls upon the filmmakers to do their upmost in using their talent to avoid making this an invitation to theft and violence.'[78] Dassin and his production team clearly had nothing to worry about if de Segogne could so seriously misconstrue the moral intention of *Du rififi chez les hommes*. It was surely safe to assume that if Tony's gang were to fail so dramatically in their plan, despite all their carefully coordinated efforts, that the film's audience was hardly going to risk such a similar heist!

## Notes

1    Artef was a Yiddish acronym for Arbeter Teater Farband (Workers' Theater Union). For more on the cultural significance of Artef, see Edna Nahshon, *Yiddish Proletarian Theatre: The Art and Politics of the Artef, 1925–1940* (Westport, CT: Greenwood Press, 1998).
2    See Saverio Giovacchini, Hollywood Modernism: Film and Politics in the *Age of the New Deal* (Philadelphia: Temple University Press, 2001). For scholarly work on the wider history of the cultural influence of European émigrés in Hollywood, see, for example, Michel Boujut and Jules Chancel, *Europe-Hollywood et retour: cinémas sous influences* (Paris: Autrement, 1986); Philip Alan Cecchittini and Don Whittemore, *Passport to Hollywood: Film Immigrants Anthology* (New York: McGraw-Hill, 1976); Jan Christopher Horak, *Fluchtpunkt Hollywood: Eine Dokumentation zur Filmemigration nach 1933* (Münster: MafS, 1984); Dominique Lebrun, *Paris-Hollywood: les français dans le cinéma américain* (Paris: Hazan, 1987); James Morrison, *Passport to Hollywood: Hollywood Films, European Directors* (Albany: SUNY Press, 1998) and Alastair Phillips and Ginette Vincendeau (eds) *Journeys of Desire: European Actors in Hollywood* (London: British Film Institute, 2006).
3    For more on Mark Hellinger, see Jim Bishop, *The Mark Hellinger Story: A Biography of Broadway and Hollywood* (New York: Appleton-Century-Crofts, 1952).
4    For an informative and much more detailed discussion of *The Naked City*, see Edward Dimendberg (2004) pp. 47–77.
5    *Combat*, 17 May 1949, quoted in Siclier and Levy (1986) p. 18.
6    *Le Parisien libéré*, 18 May 1949, quoted in Siclier and Levy (1986) p. 18.
7    When French situationist Guy Debord coined the term 'psychogeography' and published the map of his wanderings in Paris in 1957, he called the book *The Naked City* in honour of Weegee's photographs and Dassin's film. See James Naremore (1998) p. 284.
8    'The Hollywood Ten' were originally eleven in number. Bertolt Brecht answered questions and then returned immediately to East Germany. The

others who did not testify and who were subsequently punished were Alvah Bessie; Herbert Biberman; Lester Cole; Edward Dmytryk; Ring Lardner, Jr; John Howard Lawson; Albert Maltz; Samuel Ornintz; Adrian Scott and Dalton Trumbo. Only Dmytryk later recanted and in 1951, the director of the film noirs *Murder, My Sweet* (1944) and *Crossfire* (1947) agreed to cooperate and name names, including Jules Dassin. For more on HUAC, including its subsequent activities between 1951 and 1954, which led to a further list of 324 names of present and former Hollywood workers, see Paul Buhle and Dave Wagner (2003); Larry Ceplair and Steven Englund (1983); and Patrick McGilligan and Paul Buhle (1997). Naremore (1998) has an interesting chapter on the specific intersection between 'the Hollywood Blacklist' and American film noir, pp. 96–135.

9   Audio commentary by Glenn Erickson on DVD release of *Night and the City* (Criterion Publishing, 2005).
10  The film was to be an adaptation of the blacklisted Albert Maltz's novel, *The Journey of Simon McKeever*.
11  See video interview with Jules Dassin on DVD release of *Night and the City* (Criterion Publishing, 2005).
12  The film, a French-Italian co-production, was eventually directed by Julien Duvivier and first released in the USA in a French version with English subtitles before being distributed in a dubbed English language version narrated by Orson Welles.
13  Frank Tuttle is best known for being the director of the early film noir, *This Gun for Hire* (1942), which was an adaptation by Albert Maltz of Graham Greene's novel of the same name.
14  For example, McGilligan and Buhle (1997) p. 212.
15  The film was eventually completed by Henri Verneuil.
16  Luis Buñuel filmed the latter in 1956.
17  For an elegant and detailed genealogy of poetic realism, see Dudley Andrew, *Mists of Regret* (Princeton, Princeton University Press, 1995).
18  *Le Temps*, 14 January 1939, page unknown.
19  Charles O'Brien (1996) p. 8.
20  Ibid., p. 8.
21  Nino Frank, 'Un nouveau genre policier: l'aventure criminelle', *L'Ecran français*, 61 (August 1946) and Jean-Pierre Chartier, 'Les Américains aussi font des films noirs', *La Revue du cinema*, 2 (November 1946).
22  Jean-Pierre Chartier, in Silver and Ursini (1999) p. 23.
23  Nino Frank, in Silver and Ursini (1999) p. 18.
24  Ibid., p. 18.
25  Borde and Chaumeton (2002 edition) p. 92.
26  Ibid., p. 92.
27  Ibid., p. 127.
28  Ibid., p. 130.
29  And subject of another title in this series: Susan Hayward, *Les Diaboliques* (London: I.B.Tauris, 2005).
30  See Ginette Vincendeau, in Spicer (2007) pp. 32–5.
31  Ibid., p. 29.
32  Ibid., p. 33.
33  Ibid., p. 31.
34  Guérif, p. 101.

35  Ginette Vincendeau, in Spicer (2007) p. 38.
36  Claire Gorrara (2003) p. 12.
37  Ginette Vincendeau (2003) p. 100.
38  Ibid., p. 101.
39  Marcel Duhamel, 'Série Noire manifesto', http://www.gallimard.fr/catalog/html/actu/serienoire_cit.htm (accessed 20 September 2006).
40  Claire Gorrara (2003) p. 13. The celebrated crime novelist Léo Malet wrote two novels for the series, for example, under the pseudonyms of Franck Harding and Léo Latimer. See 'A l'ombre du polar', http://www.polars.org/article31.html (accessed 16 September 2007).
41  Marcel Duhamel, 'Série Noire manifesto', http://www.gallimard.fr/catalog/html/actu/serienoire_cit.htm (accessed 20 September 2006).
42  The poet, Jacques Prévert, had a significant influence on classical French cinema. He worked on scripts for several Marcel Carné films, including *Le Quai des brumes*, *Le Jour se lève* and *Les Enfants du paradis*, but he also collaborated with other notable directors, such as Jean Grémillon (*Remorques*, 1941); Jean Renoir (*Le Crime de Monsieur Lange*); Richard Pottier (*27 Rue de la Paix*, 1937) and Christian-Jaque (*Les Disparus de Saint-Agil*, 1938).
43  Of course, Raymond Chandler was actually British, but his chosen idiom in the USA was of the hard-boiled American crime writer. It is worth noting the fertile historical relationship between French cinema and many of these authors. Pierre Chenal directed the first adaptation of James M. Cain's *The Postman Always Rings Twice/Le Dernier tournant* in 1939. Jim Thompson adaptations include *Série noire* (Alain Corneau, 1979) and *Coup de torchon* (Bertrand Tavernier, 1981). David L. Goodis adaptations include *Tirez sur le pianiste* (François Truffaut, 1960), *Le Casse* (Henri Verneuil, 1971), *La Lune dans le caniveau* (Jean-Jacques Beinix, 1983), *Rue barbare* (Gilles Béhat, 1984) and *Descente aux enfers* (Francis Girod, 1986). Horace McRoy's *No Pockets in a Shroud* was adapted as *Un Linceul n'a pas de poches* (Jean-Pierre Mocky, 1974).
44  The poet, novelist, trumpeter, screenwriter and actor, Boris Vian, was a renowned figure in postwar Left Bank Parisian culture. Although he never actually visited the United States, his work was permeated with an awareness of the central place that popular American culture occupied in the cultural imagination of his French metropolitan audience. When it was originally published in 1947, Vian initially claimed that *J'irai cracher sur vos tombes* (*I Spit on Your Graves*) was only the French translation by him of an original American source novel written by Vernon Sullivan. The following year, once the book had become a bestseller, he was forced to 'come clean' about this hoax.
45  Ginette Vincendeau (2003) pp. 101–2.
46  Claire Gorrara (2003) p. 36.
47  Ibid.
48  Such was the success of *Touchez pas au grisbi* that it sold out of its initial print run less than a month after its publication on 3 January 1953. See Albert Simonin interview, *Les Cahiers de la cinémathèque*, 25 (1978) pp. 120–1.
49  The film of *Razzia sur la chnouf* was released on 7 April and *Du rififi chez les hommes* on 14 April 1955.
50  Claire Gorrara (2003) p. 9.
51  Auguste Le Breton (1981) p. 183.
52  See Lenny Borger: www.filmforum.org/archivedfilms/rififipress.html (accessed 30 December 2006).

53  Production file CN0658 B450 (Bifi library, Paris).

54  In his account of the genesis of the film, Lenny Borger cites Melville (in interview with Rui Nogueira) saying that Bérard had originally promised him the film, but after a six-month lapse in their relationship it turned out that Dassin had by then also been approached. Dassin wrote to Melville saying he would only go ahead if Melville replied agreeing to this, which he apparently did. Borger, however, also cites a contrary account by Dassin who has it that he only found out about Melville's preliminary involvement much later after the release of the film when he discovered that Bérard had 'double-crossed' Melville by originally promising the film to two people. See www.filmforum.org/archivedfilms/rififipress.html (accessed 30th December 2006).

55  Auguste Le Breton (1981) p. 186.

56  An Italian actor had originally been cast in the role, but he had to pull out because of last-minute contractual problems with another film.

57  It has been suggested that elements of the staging of the heist in *Du rififi chez les hommes* were actually borrowed from a famous jewellery raid in Marseilles. See Graham Hayes, in Powrie (2006) p. 73.

58  Dassin quoted in Lenny Borger: www.filmforum.org/archivedfilms/rififipress. tml (accessed 30 December 2006).

59  Ibid. It is also worth noting that the remuneration Le Breton received was almost on a par with Dassin's. Le Breton was paid one million francs for his contribution to the script, but he also pocketed 4.1 million francs in author's rights. These figures compare with the amount of six million francs received by the film's director. See Production File CN 0658 B450.

60  Revel, Renaud, 'Le "Rififi" Trente Ans Après', *Le Matin*, 17 July 1984, page unknown.

61  *La Cinématographie Française*, no. 1594, 27 November 1954, page unknown.

62  Lenny Borger: www.filmforum.org/archivedfilms/rififipress.html (accessed 30 December 2006).

63  Production File CN 0658 B450. Both Jean Servais and Carl Möhner would work again with Dassin on *Celui qui doit mourir* (1957), again produced by Henri Bérard.

64  Script SCEN0903 B273 (Bifi library, Paris).

65  Interview with Jules Dassin and Jean Servais, *Cinémonde* no. 1182, 4 April 1957, page unknown.

66  Prior to *Du rififi chez les hommes*, Auric had worked, for example, on Jean Cocteau's *Orphée* (1949); Charles Crichton's Ealing Studios' *The Lavender Hill Mob* (1951) and William Wyler's *Roman Holiday* (1953).

67  Dassin quoted in Borger, Lenny: www.filmforum.org/archivedfilms/rififipress.html (accessed 30 December 2006).

68  Agostini was paid 1.44 million francs for his work on the production. (Production File CN 0658 B450). According to Dassin, he was the reason so many of the technical wished to work on the production. See video interview with Jules Dassin on DVD release of *Du rififi chez les hommes* (Criterion Publishing, 2001).

69  For more on Curt Courant, see Alastair Phillips (2004).

70  Ginette Vincendeau (1992) p. 72.

71  *Arts*, 15 December 1954, page unknown. Truffaut's characteristically perceptive writing includes an account of the filming of the sequence at the Port-

Royal metro station in which he is impressed by the discretion and attentiveness of Dassin and Agostini's camerawork.

72   See video interview with Jules Dassin on DVD release of *Du rififi chez les hommes* (Criterion Publishing, 2001).

73   See interview with Jules Dassin and Jean Servais, *Cinémonde*, no. 1182, 4 April 1957, page unknown.

74   Production File CN 0658 B450 (Bifi library, Paris). The film finally came in at 129.248 million francs.

75   Ibid.

76   Ibid.

77   *Le Film Français*, 540–41 (Autumn 1954), page unknown.

78   Letter dated 1 October 1954. Production File CN 0658 B450 (Bifi library, Paris).

# 2  Reading *Rififi*

## Beginnings

We have seen that *Du rififi chez les hommes* was initially designed to have the same success with French filmgoers as Jacques Becker's profitable underworld drama, *Touchez pas au grisbi*. As already noted, the two films both had ageing male gangsters as lead characters and they shared a similar milieu of Montmartre nightclubs, gangland apartments and night-time Parisian streets. However, they differed in one significant aspect. In Becker's film, we never see the heist itself. The film is simply concerned with the robbery's troubled aftermath. In Dassin's formative take on the heist film, meanwhile, the robbery is significantly foregrounded to the extent that the film can be legitimately divided into three parts: the opening section, which establishes a psychological portrait of the thieves by detailing their extensive preparations for their planned raid on the jewellers; the concentrated middle sequence, which depicts the actual crime in painstaking and nail-biting detail and then, finally, the lengthy third act, which reveals César's betrayal of the gang and the consequences of this for both the criminal 'family' of the gangsters and the domestic family of Jo, his wife and son.

The first and last sections of the film therefore differ quite significantly from each other in terms of their treatment of narrative space and *mise-en-scène*. The opening is more measured and centred on a number of key sites of action – the café owned by Fredo where the heist is initiated; the gang's base where the details of the robbery are planned; the L'Age d'Or nightclub now run by the Grutter clan and the place where César meets Viviane; Jo's apartment in Belleville and, of course, the area around Mappin & Webb, the jewellers on Rue de la Paix in the wealthy first arrondissement where the robbery will take place. The rhythm of the third part of the film, on the other hand, is brisker, the camerawork more mobile and the treatment of spatial relations less dependent on set-design as events unravel. The lengths of the shots are shortened and Dassin increasingly intercuts between different spaces to propel the narrative forward. There is a reduction in the use of the conventional generic locations of the gangster film and a greater concentration on location cinematography not only within central Paris, but also on the rural outskirts of the city. This sense of narrative unfurling and, for the protagonists, a growing lack of command over their circumstances and their individual destinies, is strikingly different from the enclosed and concentrated visual and temporal precision of the middle scenes inside the jewellers.

In the early stages of *Du rififi chez les hommes*, Dassin deliberately concentrates our attention on the character differences between the four main gang members. This is to heighten the suspense about the way the robbery is carried out and to anticipate why the men act the way they do when things go wrong. Jo is the most youthful and virile of the four. With his modest family home and clearly expressed love for his young son, he appears, along with his wife Louise, to occupy the film's moral centre of gravity. In this sense, his role as Tony's protégé is different from that of the relationship between the younger Riton and the older Max in *Touchez pas au grisbi* – a film that lacks the explicit social conscience of Dassin's in a number of ways. The third part of *Du rififi chez les hommes*, as we shall see, for instance, openly questions the lineage established between Tony and Jo since it exposes the futility of Tony's career and then goes on to parody the legacy of violence their relationship has involved by contrasting Jo's vicious murder with his young son gleefully shooting his cowboy pistol in the air. If Jo is in some way an idealized image of heterosexual masculinity, Tony then is its antitheses. An air of fatigue compounds his melancholic and taciturn manner. He has a troubling recurrent cough, which signals further physical decline. Tony does not have a stable domestic life and his previous romantic relationship with Mado is only alluded to through an ironic photograph of the happy couple at play in a nightclub, which is presented in close-up to the spectator at the very moment he beats her off-screen. The only strength that Tony le Stéphanois exerts rests in his psychological authority as a past master of the game and, in this role, he also differs from the two remaining gang members, Mario and César.

Mario is a voluble and charismatic Italian whose physical prowess is signalled by his repeated instruction to his girlfriend, Ida, to retire to the bedroom 'to keep the bed warm'. His impulsiveness is seen in counterpoint to Tony's weary caution. Immediately after the scene in which Tony beats Mado's back, for example, Dassin immediately shows Mario, naked in his bath, having his own back playfully slapped with a bath sponge by Ida. The contrast here is not just behavioural. It illuminates Mario's sexual vitality as a force that is diametrically opposed to the disgust felt by Tony after his sexually motivated 'revenge' on Mado. Indeed, it is arguably Tony's self-loathing that serves as his final motivation for actually taking up the offer of the heist. César, the final gang member, also says little. His manner and demeanour are precise – he compares Tony with a tramp because of his dishevelled appearance – but his fastidious character is

Tony and Mado: a past never recaptured

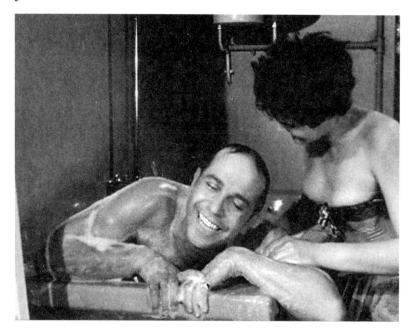

Mario and Ida: life led in the present

'There is no woman that César can resist': César (right) gazes at Viviane

presented as 'flawed' because of an almost perversely childlike sexual attraction to the singer, Viviane. 'There's no woman that César can resist,' Mario suggests mockingly. Furthermore, one could also say that César is 'feminized' in relation to the other men because of his over-stated elegance. Later on, this will have repercussions for the film's treatment of gender politics in that his character is punished in part for possessing these specific traits.

*Du rififi chez les hommes* thus relies deftly on a process of dramatic alternation and this can be examined in more detail by looking at the very beginning of the film. It starts with a close-up of a gambling table with four sets of hands managing their cards, money and drinks. We hear the on-screen sound of cards being dealt and the odd verbal command off-screen. Dassin holds this image for some time so as to intensify this study of masculine concentration. The shot thus serves as a *mise-en-abîme* for the tense and uneasy camaraderie that exists between the four gang members during the forthcoming heist sequence.

When the men around the table, including Tony who is losing the round, are finally seen in medium long-shot, the lighting is low and

A life of chance: the gambling den

noirish; the visual treatment of the milieu reminiscent of an American crime film. As Tony rises to make a call by the doorway, there is a dissolve to Jo's apartment with the young Tonio running to the edge of the sofa on which his father is reclining with the newspaper. The point in the image at which the boy places a coat hanger on Jo's foot is identical to the place of Tony within the preceding shot composition. The two, linked by name, have therefore also been linked in space and time. But, furthermore, the eye that Dassin repeatedly reveals for gesture and telling detail throughout the film, also suggests a metaphorical dimension. Jo is about to be trapped by Tony.

While Jo rearranges himself the other way round on the sofa, his line of vision is now aligned with Tonio's as the pair face Louise emerging from the kitchen with her vacuum cleaner. Every surface of the lounge is brighter and more evenly lit than the gangsters' den. As part of the conventional politics of the film, this is a clearly feminized space but it is also, as we shall see by the end, a safer one for all concerned. For the spectator watching the film a second time, this point is clearly reinforced by the intrusion of the telephone. Unlike the dramatic occasion towards

A life of security: the home

the film's conclusion when Tony rings and tragically finds Jo not there (thus being unable to warn him that he is in mortal danger), Jo here is available to talk.

When we return to the card game, the others exclude Tony, so he slowly rises from his chair to make his way to a pool table on the right. The camera follows this move in a similarly languid manner. There is an abrupt cut to a view from inside a café of a speeding car and, as the camera sharply pans rightwards to follow it come to a halt outside, the contrast is clearly made between the fatigue of Tony's body and the efficiency of the vehicle. As Fredo, the café proprietor, lifts his awning, we see Jo run onto the scene from the car. Its owner is thus concisely associated with the vigour of both youthfulness and modernity.[1]

What is also interesting here is the establishment of another significant pattern of alternation – an alternation between what might be called a French and an American system of generic representation. If the backroom that Jo now enters is marked by its similarities with any number of American gangster films, perhaps especially the one in John Huston's *The Asphalt Jungle*, the café, with its various French bottles and drinks signs, is coded specifically in European terms. This is no truer than in the *mise-en-scène* of a subsequent shot with Jo and Tony standing to the right of a poster map of France that is sponsored by the iconic French aperitif, Dubonnet. It is not too far-fetched thus to see a maternal analogy being drawn between the map and the figure of Suzanne, Fredo's elderly wife, for she explicitly enters the frame at this point and seems to stand deliberately in front of the document on the wall. Suzanne will turn out to be the main source of comfort to Louise when the Grutters kidnap the young Tonio. When Jo and Tony leave the café and enter the daylight of the Paris streets, this nurturing aspect of nationhood is reinforced by Jo who suggests 'Get out to the country. Get some air in your lungs.' In retrospect, in view of what happens at the Grutters' rural villa in St Rémy les Chevreuse, this turns out to be ironic advice.

So far, we have seen two telling instances of the visual play between internal and external space. There is another in the café to which Jo and Tony now decamp and, again, there is a reiteration of the significance of Frenchness within an international context. Mario has now joined the pair and they sit down with their coffees in front of a tripartite window that overlooks a street corner.[2] As the reason for their meeting becomes clear, the men recoil from their huddle and lean back. This communal gesture allows the camera to zoom in, as if it were actually moving 'through' the central glass panel, to the shop front across the road. The shop belongs to the British jewellery firm, Mappin & Webb.[3] 'Webb' says Tony, 'You're crazy. Why not the Bank of France?' This would be more appropriate certainly for a scene in which the men are beginning to plan a robbery over croissants, but it is noticeable that the site of their attention is explicitly not French. The scene is set in one of the most cosmopolitan spaces of central Paris: the area around Place Vendôme, which was then and still is a destination for international tourists and business travellers seeking luxury goods from not just France but around the world. It therefore features, among other things, as a place apart from the Parisian working-class everydayness of the world that Jo, especially, ordinarily inhabits in the northeastern section of the capital.

This is to outline the sociological significance of the narrative moment, but the scene contains other repercussions that relate both to the drama that will ensue and to the potential of seeing *Du rififi chez les hommes* as a

Planning the robbery

transnational film noir. Is it not relevant, for example, that the site of the robbery, like the film's director, is clearly international in character? The prominence of an Italian in the middle of two Frenchmen, and of one who through his name might even really be Swedish, underlines this tension further.[4] In his position at the apex of the triangle within the composition of the shot, and because of the aesthetic distinctiveness of his black hat, Mario thus conveys an interesting degree of cultural difference. (We may remember here that Dassin had spent time in Italy during his period of European exile.) That Dassin too was an outsider is especially revealing, for it relates to the final sense at stake within the complicated spatial/viewing relations of this sequence. As we have seen, the camera seems to move effortlessly 'through' the café glass to the jewellers to initiate the significance of the building to the drama. This degree of instantaneous transparency is, necessarily, the very opposite of what it will really take to crack the interior of the business from outside. Moreover, the idea of entering something from the outside simultaneously provokes the possibility of reading the act of 'breaking in' in connection with what was clearly a formative moment for Dassin. The cracking open of the safe within might also be seen (retrospectively) as a metaphor for his attempts, as an American director of film noir, to unlock and master the codes of French genre cinema as a springboard to a successful European film career. And so it is to this central part of *Du rififi chez les hommes* – the heist – that we shall now turn.

### *Du rififi chez les hommes* and the aesthetics of the heist thriller

*Du rififi chez les hommes* has justifiably been celebrated over the years for its influence on the heist thriller as an international cinematic genre. As Ginette Vincendeau has pointed out, the figure of the 'clean' safebreaker has an especially longstanding pedigree within the history of the French narrative representation of crime. Going back to the figure of the *'gentleman-cambrioleur'* such as Arsène Lupin, she argues, 'safebreakers [have consistently constituted] the aristocracy of hoodlums.'[5] This nominal air of 'respectability' is culturally significant in the case of Dassin's film for two reasons: first, it allows the more sordid and despicable crimes of drug-peddling and pimping to be aligned with the ugly, more contemporary, immorality of the Grutters and then, secondly, as we shall later see, it also explicitly displaces prostitution (and thus untrustworthiness) onto the figure of the female, rather than male, protagonists.

The spectatorial pleasures of the heist film are imbricated within a perverse system of approval and validation for what is essentially a profoundly illegitimate act. The greater the concentration on psychological detail and the mental and physical effort behind the act of crime, the greater the degree of empathy one has with the villains. In *Du rififi chez les hommes*, this process reaches a kind of apogee; we simply want the four men to get away with it. One of the reasons for this may be the very precise correlation between the attentive, careful visual style of the robbery sequence and the robbery itself. In other words, there is an intrinsically meta-textual symbiosis between the élan of the filmmaking and the élan of the safebreaking.

The initial planning of the robbery is detailed in a systematic and highly economical fashion through an elliptical montage of various sequences that briefly explain to the spectator how the gang members case the jewellers' shop in order to anticipate and solve the problems they will encounter in the actual process of the heist. What we therefore see is a compressed temporal and spatial version of the raid – a rehearsal of sorts – so that when it is actually played out in a more extended version the second time around, the sense of watching a calculated private performance is cleverly exacerbated. Part of the tension of watching the robbery thus comes as much from scrutinizing the qualities of the narrative action – checking that things go according to plan – as anticipating the results these qualities are designed to achieve.

The men first decide to go for the safe, which they know is at the back of the shop, rather than the goods on display in the window. Jo and Tony go back to the street and memorize the names and locations of all the surrounding businesses. These become, in part, an artful microcosm of the locations Dassin has recently inhabited as an international filmmaker. We are told, for example, that the Parisian silk merchant, Henri Maupiou, opposite Mappin & Webb, has branches in London and New York. As the pair progress up the street, the Kodak-Pathé shop comes closer to the fore.

Its Franco-American brand neatly condenses the twin identities of the film's director.

The gangsters then rent a hotel room across the street and in a scene that bears close similarities with Robert Wise's later heist thriller, *Odds Against Tomorrow* (1959), they carefully time all the things that routinely happen in the neighbourhood outside during the proposed hours of the robbery. Mario takes an imprint of the key into the apartment above the shop and they calculate the duration of the getaway car's journey from its hiding place to the place where it will be needed. This section of the film has a powerful musical score provided by George Auric, which closely conforms to the generic conventions of the urban thriller. There is a minimal amount of dialogue: just the diegetic sounds of the key in the lock, the footsteps of the security guard and the engine of the stylish Renault belonging to the gang. Next, we see César visit the shop by day to identify the location of the safe and the nature of the business's security system. The gang then sets about planning how to deal with eliminating the sound of the wired alarm. They hit upon the idea of using the foam from a fire extinguisher to prevent the alarm being heard during the vital

Mapping the Rue de la Paix in Paris

moments: 45 minutes into the film, they are now ready to put their plan into action.

The extended sequence from the four arriving outside Mappin & Webb at night to the end of the raid and the shot of the getaway car leaving Rue de la Paix occupies a full 25 minutes of screen time. Throughout, there is no dialogue and no non-diegetic music at all. It is an extraordinary feat of filmmaking and the most Bazinian section of the film in terms of there being a pronounced observational style that is heavily reliant on the long take and an almost phenomenological interest in the unfurling of real time. Vision and time are indeed specifically foregrounded in a number of ways. First, for example, there is the extensive detailing of the way in which the two concièrges are blindfolded in the darkness above their flat. Here, long mobile shots, illuminated only by torchlight, show how the couple are denied sight just at the point when the gang members begin successfully to visualize their way around the luxuriously decorated living room for the first time. Narrative space, in this early part of the film, is only broken up to show simultaneous action or, especially importantly, the revelation of a telling close-up detail such as the progress of the uncovering of the parquet floor.

The second, and arguably most important, aspect of the film's handling of vision and time rests in the way it provides a template for how popular cinema should treat the aesthetics of the heist genre. Here, the central points of tension for the thieves are clearly temporal and spatial. We are constantly being made aware, for instance, of the process of time passing and the significance of the impending deadline of dawn – of time literally running out. Dassin does this by focusing closely on the gang members' watches and also by intercutting between these shots and images of the clock downstairs in the shop. Similarly, we are also reminded that the success of the theft depends on the necessity of not actually being seen, of remaining invisible inside to the outside world. Dassin excels by relaying this to us at the very outset by showing the process of the blackout of the windows by heavy curtain material, but he continues to make the point throughout by identifying internal and external spatial relations in terms of what can and what can not be seen by whom and at what point in time this dichotomy specifically occurs.

There are two crucial examples of this narrative method. We have been watching the gang work for some time in penetrating the floor/

ceiling to gain access to the shop below their feet. The horizontal surface of the tiles and then the opening up of a hole through them has become a site of intense visual attention. We watch the gang seemingly float a tissue to indicate that clear air has been reached and the space has finally been breached. Dassin then cuts to the darkness of the shop floor below and thus, for the first time, the contract of spatial alignment with the thieves has been broken: we can now see what they cannot.

This becomes a matter of continual alternation and a bearer of increasing tension as we are now able to counter the risks that the gang are running more fully than they themselves can. But the system of seeing/unseen is unstable. At a vital point, when the gang begins to climb back upstairs after gathering the jewels from the safe, we see something else that most of them do not witness. César cannot resist descending briefly one more time. He seizes the very jewel that has fascinated him in the shop the previous day. This becomes the gem that sets in trail the downfall of the whole enterprise and only we know it.

If this particular example rests on a vertical pattern of up and down, another depends more on a more horizontal play between inside and

A site of intense visual attention

Breaking spatial alignment

The downfall begins

outside. The second way Dassin interrupts our cognitive engagement with
the thieves is during another moment of dramatic breakthrough. The gang
has been boring at the back of the safe for some time and has just managed
to create a hole out of which to lift the jewels. Instead of a point-of-view
shot of the gems inside, we then cut, completely unexpectedly, to two
police officers outside. We see them notice a stolen bike and car and watch
them realize that thieves are in the area. This sets up a new interrelationship between the processes of detection and of the successful
completion of the raid. The narrative tension has been ratcheted up one
step further. Not only are we left wondering if the gang will finish their
plan inside, but we are also forced to consider the fact that they may be
caught outside.

Another key aspect of the film's aesthetic interest in the act of crime
lies in the visual and aural representation of penetration. It is crucial that
this occurs twice – once in the case of the ceiling and twice in the case of
the back of the safe – for this necessarily induces a greater sense of
challenge and danger on the part of the spectator watching the action
unfurl. Dassin makes interesting comparative use of the two moments by
showing us the particular skills the individual gang members deploy.
Breaking up the floor and boring through to the ceiling below is essentially
a laborious and time-consuming task best achieved by the muscular Jo.
Opening up the safe with the aid of a technically sophisticated drilling
apparatus requires a more precise technique and this therefore suits
César's more methodical character.

Graphic pattern and the treatment of sound define both actions. The
key shape is a circle, in the latter case a mathematically perfect circle
created on the metallic surface of the safe. Constant recourse to close-ups
of round clocks, watches and faces in the *mise-en-scène* emphasizes this
motif of circularity.[6] Usually too, at the point in the sequence, the rhythm
of the editing alters and, in a fashion exemplary of the suspense film, it
becomes more rapid as we alternate from one visual element to the next.
This is especially true in the recurrent tense exchange of looks between the
men.

Sound remains a central integrated aspect in this creation of narrative tension. In the case of the first instance, it seems to be more
explicitly associated with the domestic environment upstairs. There is the

The motif of circularity: the floor

The motif of circularity: the safe

worry of leaning accidentally on the piano keys in the living room and the fact that the plasterwork and dust from the parquet slats will set off the alarm as it falls down through the hole. In the second, the sound is more mechanical and thus unnatural. The timbre of the drill against the cold metal of the safe is especially excruciating to listen to. As well as indicating the severity of the experience, it also suggests a feeling of troubled unease. Dassin's interpretation of the skills behind the enterprise as a whole therefore reinforces the pattern of alignment and narrative sympathy that have already been established in the pre-heist sequence. The gang members may work together (they wear identical white shoes[7]), but Jo's looser, more natural artisanal charm appears to be favoured over César's technocratic, even inverted, exactitude.

Dassin remains careful not simply to repeat what we have already been led to expect within the representation of the heist. He achieves a delicate balance between anticipation and innovation. Several details such as the elimination of the alarm with the fire extinguisher foam go according to plan, but new elements are also introduced such as the decision to use an inverted umbrella to prevent the debris falling onto the floor below. What

Escape into the urban everyday

both of these elements suggest is a fundamental reordering of the ordinary. A basic item such as an umbrella, for example, can be turned into a tool of crime. On the one hand, such resourcefulness is indicative of the craftsman-like nature of the proceedings, but, on the other, it is also a reminder of the subversive nature of the actual enterprise. This point is certainly emphasized by the decision constantly to contrast the closely framed studio shots from within with more expansive location shots from outside. These images, which are beautifully rendered by Philippe Agostini, are reminiscent of the kind of humanist photography by the likes of Izis, Edouard Boubat and Marcel Bovis that was then in vogue within French visual culture.[8] In particular, they deliberately seem to evoke the more mundane (and natural) details of ordinary Parisian life, such as the delivery of flowers to a florist and the cleaning of the street at dawn. It is this world of the urban everyday that will increasingly come to bear on the treatment of the film's *mise-en-scène* once the members of the gang make their escape and the perfect circle of their criminal achievement begins to break down.

## Space and genre: the nightclub

In the opening sections of *Du rififi chez les hommes*, however, the world outside impinges little on the film's narrative and there is, as already suggested, a prevalence of set design rather than location cinematography. This is especially important to the way in which the L'Age d'Or nightclub features a key site of action. Let us now look at the arrival of Tony at the club for the first time since his release from prison and the crucial song sequence that attempts to provide an interpretation of the hitherto mysterious term, 'rififi'.

That the L'Age d'Or inhabits a world apart from family life in Belleville is indicated in the slow dissolve from the front door of Jo's apartment to the entrance of the nightclub. The overt nature of this transition between domesticity and criminal glamour is visible in numerous American film noirs of the period such as Fritz Lang's then recent *The Big Heat* (1953), but in this instance, it is coded explicitly in Franco-American terms. By the time the dissolve is completed, we are able to see the fan effect of the neon 'rays' of light that frame the arched door being bordered on either side by two visiting American sailors. Montmartre had long been conventionally represented in French popular genre cinema as a nocturnal melting pot of different cultures, but as with Jean-Pierre Melville's image of an American sailor at dawn in Place Pigalle in *Bob le flambeur*, the collision of the two national signifiers is explicitly rendered to suggest the notion of an urban culture in transition.

We enter the club more or less on Tony's terms as the camera follows him descend the staircase, refuse the offer of the cloakroom attendant, and move into the space of the club to survey the dance floor. The camera rests behind his back as the spectator observes all the conventional generic trappings of this heavily mythologized space: the slow lounge music, the glamorous couples in evening gowns and dinner suits, the individual drinking tables and the subdued lighting arrangement. What stands out is the way that the low and even lighting pattern is deliberately broken up by a single mobile spotlight being manipulated by a woman on the small stairway on the opposite side of the floor. In noir fashion, it indicates that the surface aesthetic of this milieu is potentially unstable and treacherous.

Within the conventions of the American film noir, one would expect this instability to be explicitly projected onto the figure of the female protagonist to indicate her threatening status as the 'femme fatale'.[9] Despite it being a French phrase, it is worth remembering that the 'femme fatale' rarely featured as a narrative figure in French film noir and so it is that when Tony finally encounters Mado a couple of shots later, the alternating lighting setup captures them both as they shift from being caught in the shadows to being temporarily illuminated in a halo effect. The lighting here thus simultaneously evokes the flickering of their rekindled sexual desire and the dissipated nature of their relationship. Their romance is either about to recommence or burn out entirely. The exchange of looks between the two intensifies and the choice of alternating high and low angles to indicate their respective seated and standing positions seems to encompass an unhealthily uneven set of power relations that will be born out in the subsequent sequence showing Tony's brutality towards his former girlfriend. Again, unlike the case of American film noir at points of on-screen sexual tension, the male figure rests in complete mastery of the look.

The question of looking and sexual relations is a central aspect of the way in which the film subsequently visualizes the song 'Rififi', sung by Viviane, during a second visit to the L'Age d'Or. This sequence begins with a strikingly different view of the club from a hidden window in a first-floor office above the dining tables and dance floor. In a manner similar to other American film noirs with a nightclub background such as *Gilda* (Charles Vidor, 1946), as well as *Touchez pas au grisbi*, this privileged view is one that belongs to the criminal gangland  patron; in this case, Pierre Grutter rather than Ballin Munsdon (George Macready). We see a hand reach forward and abruptly close the curtain. This degree of control over what gets seen and not seen appears to set up a similar spatial and visual chain to that explored previously in relation to the heist. In a sense, the Grutters' occupation of the L'Age d'Or is indeed like that of Tony's gang's takeover of the two floors of the bank building. Both depend on a sense of divided internal space and both depend on the matter of close surveillance. The ensuing violent exchange between the ruthless Pierre and his younger brother Rémi reinforces this duality as we bear in mind that only seconds before we have seen an important transitional conversation between the older Tony and younger Jo on the Rue de la Paix. Whereas the generational interrelationship between the latter seems stable, considered and mutually respectful, here Pierre ridicules his younger drug-addicted sibling as he pleads for relief from his cravings. Pierre is then shown locking the 'safe' of his office drawer where he keeps the drugs. Unlike the safe at Mappin & Webb, it is never going to be cracked.

The sequence moves downstairs as we follow three of Tony's gang members to their seats. One of the hostesses asks Jo his name and he replies 'Maximilian'. This is surely a humorous reference to both the name of the principal protagonist in *Touchez pas au grisbi*, Max, and the star persona of the actor Jean Gabin, who played the lead role in the film. Dassin, as we have already seen, was all too aware that *Du rififi chez les hommes* lacked any such glamour – Jo is no Max and Carl Möhner is clearly no Jean Gabin – but he was not averse to citing its influential predecessor for playful ends. Jo's deliberate deceit has another function as well. It sets up the issues of naming and cinematic intertextuality with which Viviane's song explicitly deals. In this sense, we are thus being told from the very outset, the film's 'number' is more than just a conventional opportunity for sexual display and musical entertainment. It can also be seen to relate to the way in which Dassin explores his film's own sense of inheritance concerning the representation of crime, violence and sexuality within film noir.

The song is an attempt to explain to the audience what 'rififi' actually means. What did 'rififi' first imply for Auguste Le Breton, the man who appears to have coined the phrase? Beyond a general sense of criminal violence and trouble, we cannot be sure, but it is likely that the etymology of the word relates to the original references made to North African criminals in his source novel. The Riffs or Riffis were Moroccan Berbers whose leader, Abd el-Krim, fought against Spanish and French colonial rule in northern Morocco. In 1921, he had established the republic of the Rif.[10] It is also worth mentioning that 'rififi' sounds like the Italian slang word for fire, '*ruffo*'. The actual alliterative sound of the word mattered too. It resembles the rat-a-tat-tat of gunfire as the synergy between Viviane's voice and the shots of a gun at the end of the song make clear. No matter, Viviane's unfolding explanation is less precise and, given that her presentation depends on the depiction of different layers of visual reality, we are clearly encouraged to view it as being unstable and prone to heavy mythologization. In short, 'rififi' and what it might signify is based on performance.

Viviane's 'number' is staged in three parts and is divided in terms of its address to both the cinematic screen behind her and the theatrical audience in front. Her voice and body thus serve to mediate between these two worlds. The performance begins with a seemingly impossible image of a larger-than-life spinning silhouette of a male gangster. He fills the foreground of a photographic representation of an illuminated city street receding into the distance. As the body turns, it begins to diminish in scale just at the point that Viviane herself enters the stage facing the image with her arms outstretched and with her back to the audience. The camera is positioned to the left so that a visual dialogue is established allowing the cinematic spectator to assess the relationship between Viviane's words and gestures and the silent routine of her male co-performer. It seems that the lithe and mobile male gangster is there to illustrate the words of the song. When Viviane refers to his propensity to resolve issues with violence, for instance, we see the man cradle his gun. When she turns and runs to the screen saying that she's next in line for 'rififi', the silhouette actually appears to strike her, breaking the physical illusion of a separation between the two levels of representation.

At this point, there is a cut and the singer turns to face the audience to 'speak' to them. As she progresses with her explanation, she moves to Jo and the hostess on the right of the image. At the moment when the orchestra reprise the word through instrumentation alone, Dassin cuts to an image of César and Mario on the left admiring her. Viviane comes over to them saying that that you won't find 'rififi' in the dictionary. Again, there is a cut to the same two-shot on the musical echo. César is now under her spell. His obviously phallic cigarette has to be discretely removed from his mouth by his male companion. The foregrounding of César's attraction to Viviane in this staged way is significant for, as we shall later see, the strength of his desire leads eventually to his own violent demise in the venue he first met her.

In many ways, Viviane's song mediates some of the wider representational issues in the film, along with providing an explanation for the meaning of the film's title. It is as if the wider politics of criminal violence and commercial sexuality become 'safely' rendered through the displacement of the real world by the world of theatricality. If César's sexual desire at this point in the action aligns him with the position of being Viviane's client, we are also invited to see similarities between the singer and her screen pimp/object of desire and the former relationship between Tony and Mado (both of whom are actually absent at that point in the nightclub audience). Crucially, what we are never allowed to see properly in the previous scenes offstage, gets played out in an exaggerated if nonetheless disturbing set of gestures and glances. The point here though is that the dynamic between the two performers is prominently physical – the male gangster is impossibly athletic – whereas Tony's present-day persona has all the vitality drained out of him. The dandified object of attention on screen is performing an ideal that the real-life gangster can barely live up to. Furthermore, the strength and vitality of Magali Noël's performance eclipses the relatively passive position that Mado has been given up to now within the diegesis. She is

'Rififi' Part One

'Rififi' Part Two

'Rififi' Part Three

thus able to articulate what Mado would once have said, but through bitter experience would never dream of saying now.

If we proceed with this level of disparity between the real and the mythical, we can begin to see how Viviane's song is more than just a highly unpleasant rendering of the ways in which women figure in the world of 'rififi'. Its play on different orders of reality suggests a degree of trickery and lack of substance. The song may even be seen as some kind of warning. In the second part of the 'number', for instance, Viviane actually 'enters' the film that has been playing behind her. After having disappeared behind the curtain, she emerges as a silhouette partnering the gangster we are now explicitly told is her patron. 'When I am done working the beat, he takes me to the movies as a treat,' she explains as the pair appears to walk in tandem down the street. He does not care what kind of film they see as long as it has got 'rififi' in it. Is she telling the 'real' gangsters in the audience that their lives are an illusion, that they are living a false ideal bound up in cinematic myth rather than in the real world? If this were true, we still have to reconcile the singer's apparent authority with the degree of misogyny that, so typical of the time, permeates the film. What is so disturbing to the contemporary spectator is that Viviane then also goes on to relay what it is like to be the female partner of such men when they return home from watching such a spectacle and re-enact its fantasies on their women. After a mannered display of the kind of physical violence that has previously been disavowed and left off-screen, the singer even reminds us of her own complicity. In another unsettling analogy between the narrative of the performance and the narrative of Dassin's film, Viviane tells us that 'rififi' is the price she will pay for the 'paradise' she desires. Her lack of physical substance – all she is here is silhouette – thus also becomes a mirror for the insubstantial and treacherous role she will play in reality later on in the film when she inadvertently betrays Tony's gang to the Grutters.

By the beginning of the third section of the song, Viviane is back on the steps of the rostrum. The dialogue between her outstretched body, the action on the screen behind and the response of the diegetic audience continues, but its decoupage is more managed in a succession of briefer, closer shots that bear no relation to any point of view other than the artificial one imposed by the film's director (and thus shared by the cinematic spectator). Indeed, the intimate scale of the final two images of the screen gangster and the theatrical performer, as well as the almost possessed tonality of Viviane's concluding notes of the song, suggest a degree of mutual self-absorption that excludes any sense of knowledge that there is a 'real world' off-screen and offstage. It is only when Tony descends the stairs and temporarily meets the singer's gaze in the subsequent shot that this sense of stylized artifice is shattered and the tragedy of the film can now properly unwind.

## Space and genre: the city

The tragedy of *Du rififi chez les hommes* is bound up with the representation of urban space, but the way Dassin pictures the streets of Paris is not consistent. The scenes leading up to the robbery, for example, represent the city largely in terms of an easygoing familiarity. The central protagonists are intimately aware of their surroundings and there is a good-humoured interrelationship between their activities and the everyday lives of the Parisians with whom they come into contact. The city is seen as a kind of familial home. In common with many French film noirs, including the then recent models of *Razzia sur la chnouf* and *Touchez pas au grisbi*, there is none of the desperation and foreboding one associates with such Hollywood film noirs as *The Asphalt Jungle* and *The Street Without Name*, both of whose titles indicate the sense of malaise that lies at the heart of their take on the American city. After the robbery, things change and there is a greater degree of detachment between characters and their environment. Although Dassin never especially indicates a degree of threat or menace, the spatial coordinates of the film become more unsettled and we begin to dispense with the previously close alignment displayed between the men and the city they inhabit.

The most 'noirish' moment in the film's *mise-en-scène* occurs just before the robbery as we see Tony just after he has left his apartment on the way to join his fellow gang members. Instead of cutting immediately to their meeting, Dassin presents two extended nocturnal shots at the Place de l'Opéra that depict Tony, alone in the city at night, stealing the car that will be used for their getaway. The first begins with a low angle medium shot of Tony in a hat and raincoat standing on some steps in front of a

The city at night

large commercial building. To his left are three bulbs from a street lamp. They provide the necessary main source of illumination. Above him and to his left, the glare of neon lettering breaks up the saturated blackness of the overall frame. As Tony moves away, the camera shifts to a more horizontal position as we see him walk across the rain soaked paving stones to a line of parked cars in the middle distance. The iconography and the tone of the image is archetypal noir. Were it not for the occasional French word visible to the more alert spectator, this could be a scene from any number of American films of the period. It is as if Tony has crossed territories.

In the next shot we see Tony nervously begin to assess his opportunities. People in evening clothes pass him and there is a brisk leftwards pan as he tries to unlock a car. Behind are more commercial buildings with illuminated signs that break up the composition and throw reflected light onto the polished black surfaces of the vehicles. The scale of the architecture and the anonymity of the milieu suggest a world away from the daytime cafés and cosy inner city apartments seen previously. By the time we finally see Tony break into a car, his silhouette at the door is far less distinct than the dazzle of neon on the car glass to his rear. In his study of the way urban space was configured within the American film noir, Edward Dimendberg argues that one feature of the way that many films represented the centres of such cities as New York and Chicago was to elicit an 'agoraphobic sensation of being overwhelmed by space' to the extent that 'fears of constriction, or the fear of losing one's way in the metropolis ... [could] generally be assumed'.[11] This brief sequence is the closest that *Du rififi chez les hommes* comes to this and provides an exception to the dominant treatment of Paris within French film noir. For just a moment, it seems as if Tony too has been swallowed by the night.

The way in which Dassin depicts Mario's funeral is typical of the shift in Parisian representation that occurs in the film after the robbery. Its more fluid, journalistic style recalls the realist treatment of New York in sections of *The Naked City*. Here, for instance, there is a predominance of long shots, which exacerbates the difference between this section and the intensive claustrophobia of the way the heist itself was visualized. This is the first part of the film since the robbery in which one has been allowed to breathe some fresh air. It is therefore significant that this is also the point in the film when the spectator is most clearly detached from any of the

Mario's funeral

principal characters. Indeed, through the opening interrogation of a police
inspector by a waiting journalist, this is the only real moment in the film that
one begins to feel the pressure of the law. Unlike the treatment of the
outcome of the heist in *The Asphalt Jungle*, which the operations of the police
increasingly dominate, Dassin's film generally allows a different sort of
morality to evolve, as if there were a greater sense of destiny involved than
the more transient one imposed by the faceless men employed by the state.

The setting is the wintry banks of the River Seine not far from the
main heart of the city. In the opening shot we see leaves falling in the
foreground as a hearse crosses a main street and comes to a halt near the
iron bridge of an overhead Métro line. We only gather that this is Mario's
funeral from listening to the conversation between the police inspector and
the journalist after an anonymous press photographer has taken their
photographs. It turns out that this is to be a typical gangland funeral: there
will be an escort of flower-laden vehicles, but not a person to be identified
since the cars will be empty bar their invisible drivers.

This is thus the first part of the film in which the world belonging to
the other side of the urban mirror that Tony and his fellow gang members

ordinarily inhabit is properly revealed. By foregrounding the absence of
these now familiar characters and the lack of presence of all the types we
have previously seen in such stylized sequences, as in the L'Age d'Or, the
film begins to evoke a more indeterminate rendering of urban space. There
is the sense that, in direct opposition to the over-determined control over
their surroundings the men exhibited during the actual robbery, the
remaining gang members' take on the world of the city is now more
provisional and less easily managed.

This is indicated, for example, in the succession of shots of the cortège
moving along the riverbank from no identifiable point of view. It is only
afterwards that our attention is drawn to a speeding taxi coming to a halt
on the bridge above the action. From a viewpoint provided only to us, and
not the police below, we see Tony and Jo pay their respects to their fallen
comrade. It is the only tightly framed shot within the sequence. The careful
distinction between the presentation of the inside and the outside of a
milieu that defined the intensive visual rhetoric of the heist is now
reconsidered. It is no longer certain who is in control and one's sense of
how the city's space may be navigated has thus been permanently
fractured.

This sense of spatial dispersal is exacerbated by the kidnap of Tonio
and by Tony's efforts to save the boy and salvage the loot that has been
stolen in the robbery. There is, for example, an increased predominance of
telephones within the *mise-en-scène* as Dassin repeatedly intercuts between
Grutter and Jo and between Tony and Jo's home. To this extent, new parts
of Paris such as the railway area around Port Royal are also shown and for
the first time in the narration we leave the city for the semi-rural area of St
Rémy les Chevreuse, where the showdown between Tony and the Grutter
clan eventually takes place. The emergence of this new pattern of cognition
required by the spectator to make sense of these interconnected locations
has the effect of breaking up the seamless flow of narrative space that has
been such a hallmark of the central section of the film.

It is interesting how the journeys to and from the villa are mediated
differently in terms of their treatment of movement. In the first
sequence, there is an emphasis on human agency and public transport.
With the complicity of Mado, whom Tony meets again on a railway
bridge, a plot is hatched to trace the location of the villa by following the

drug runner who is supplying Rémi with his fix. The drug dealer complains that his car has broken down and that he will have to take the train all the way out to the end of the line. This would be impossible in the case of the American film noir in which, in films like *On Dangerous Ground*, the distinction between urban and suburban or rural space is almost always managed through the representation of the car and the highway. Instead, here, the relationship between the city centre of Paris and its periphery is visualized in some detail by the ordinary business of entering a station, looking up a sign on a platform and catching a train. This has the effect of reinscribing the sense of everydayness that permeated the beginning of the film, but it also reinforces the crucial distinction already observed between the French and American traditions of depicting urban space in film noir. Whereas the American city was largely seen as a site of anonymity or alienation, especially in such landmark texts as *The Big Heat* and *Double Indemnity*, the French city could still be capable of being mapped by a set of navigable routes and familiar domesticated landmarks. As if to reinforce this point, Dassin subsequently chooses to use the suburban café belonging to Madame Dupré as a place of intermediary refuge where Tonio can be left while he returns to the villa to rescue Jo. Much as Suzanne becomes a surrogate maternal figure to Jo's wife at this crucial point of tension in the film, so Madame Dupré here temporarily becomes the same to Jo's son.

The return to Paris is different and here it is revealing to return again to Edward Dimendberg's description of the changing pattern of American film noir's treatment of the city. Dimendberg's argument rests on a shift in representation that he sees occurring by the 1950s. He suggests that whereas many American noirs of the 1940s such as *Scarlet Street* relied on a spatially determined 'centripetal' awareness of the city centre – navigable on foot – many films such as *Kiss Me Deadly* and *Thunder Road* (Arthur Ripley, 1958) were becoming more determined by temporality with a 'centrifugal' awareness of space that was only navigable by car. The depiction of Los Angeles in the former, for instance, revealed 'a spatial environment increasingly devoid of landmarks and centers and often likely to seem permanently in motion'.[12] Dimendberg's core argument is that this suburbanization of narrative space conveyed through an emphasis on cars, highways and new housing developments was contingent on a broader shift in American society away from the European model of city living towards something more mobile and provisional.

How does this relate to *Du rififi chez les hommes*? It certainly seems that Dassin is aware of change at the peripheries of Paris – a place like St Rémy les Chevreuse is clearly on the cusp of residential development – but he also wants to show the residual legacy of an older pattern of urban consciousness. It is thus particularly interesting to note how the car itself is used in the film. Unlike the case with the American model of noir representation, it is explicitly shown to be unnecessary in the journey away from the city; rather it is used only to show a return to Paris in which the worn and familial fold of the capital's streets is contrasted with the desolate and unfinished domestic environment of the Grutters' villa. The cinematic telling of this journey is extraordinary, not least for the way it partly seems to pre-empt the car journey to Paris made by the archetypal hybrid 'Franco-American' gangster, Michel Poiccard (Jean-Paul Belmondo), in Jean-Luc Godard's *À bout de souffle* (1960). In Dassin's version though, it is the young passenger, Tonio, dressed in cowboy costume, who is given the role of re-enacting the drama of Hollywood masculinity in a French context.

For Tonio, in his cowboy outfit, the desperate ride back is an exhilarating opportunity for play. He shoots his pistol in the air and relishes the sensation of being in the back of an open-topped car. A rapid succession of impressionistic point-of-view shots of trees and sky demonstrate a visceral sense of space and movement. If Tonio's gaze is mobile and interested in what he notices along the route as the car hurtles by, Tony's is more fixed: the swerves of the road ahead constantly threaten to destabilize him completely. The only question on our mind is whether he will make it back home or succumb to his injuries and lose control of the vehicle. In the heist sequence, Dassin's control over visual space was rigidly managed and defined by the intersection of relatively static horizontal and vertical planes of action. Here one has the opposite. There is no definition. Space is chaotic, shifting and surreal. The images eventually contain nothing more than edges of buildings or lampposts flashing by. The asphalt turns into a blur. Even the image of the majestic Arc de Triomphe seems to act in cruel counterpoint to the desperation of the wounded Tony. He only just makes it home.

Tony's final journey

Tonio: an exhilarating opportunity for play

Space is chaotic, shifting and surreal

## Men and trouble

It is no coincidence that *Du rififi chez les hommes* ends with the death of Tony at the very point that Tonio is returned to his mother and the police begin to unpick the contents of the car. This is the moment when the consequence of the interrelationship between the different family structures in the film is made most apparent. The rivalry between the all-male 'family' of thieves and the Grutters has led to the deaths of Tony, Jo, César and Mario (not to mention the main members of the Grutter family) and this means, in particular, that the young Tonio is now bereft of a father. The only remaining family unit in the film is thus one that will be predominately managed by women. In this sense, Dassin's film seemingly ends with a return to conventional femininity and the home.

The French gangster film genre, like its American counterpart, was marked by a repeated decision to relegate women characters to the peripheries of the narrative action. As has already been argued, this marginalization is represented in *Du rififi chez les hommes* by a desire to depict the female sphere as something either excessively performative (in the case of Viviane) or tangential to the main plot's concentration on the coordination of male camaraderie (in the cases of Mado, Louise and Ida). Even the 'femininized' César gets his final comeuppance. As Noël Burch and Geneviève Sellier have suggested more generally in relation to postwar French cinema, this tendency echoed the way in which female characters were repeatedly vilified or punished in films of the time in a move conceived to reassert a more virile representation of French masculinity following the compromised image of wartime 'male defeat'.[13] The central part of the film's dramatic logic is thus ferociously masculine to the point of being 'homosocial' in terms of its attention to men's emotional affiliations, repeated eyeline matches and the mutual occupation of an intensely restricted series of shot frames.

Writing of the legacy of this formative kind of visual attention within the subsequent gangster films of Jean-Pierre Melville, Ginette Vincendeau has suggested that in 'Melville's understated universe, the heist actually becomes the stage for a display of masculinity in motion'.[14] 'We admire the men for their skills so much,' she suggests, 'that we forget they deploy them in the service of crime. This is because the heist mobilizes the most noble kind of work: that of the superior artisan. ... Heists also require total attention and coordination with other men, and therefore trust. ... [Indeed,] professional skills are a core element of male bonding.'[15] All of this is certainly true in relation to Dassin's film as well, but only up to a point.

Vincendeau's emphasis on the skilfulness and masculine solidarity expressed by the act of crime is convincing in that it points to a shift in later postwar French representation towards a harder more 'technocratic' version of society in which the spectator is invited to perceive a degree of similarity between the efficiency of the new white-collar *cadre* and the spruce, clinically effective gangsters of Melville's fictional universe.[16] In this world, she suggests, to use Kristin Ross's formulation, 'Technology – cars, guns – can be harnessed by men, but it is harnessed in order to erase all the more effectively the [new] feminine-orientated technologies that contribute[d] to the "colonization of everyday life".'[17] What is interesting though in *Du rififi chez les hommes* is how Dassin seems to negotiate a place somewhere between an acknowledgement of these processes (and the 'threat of femininity' that they contained) and the legacy of the more socially conscious set of crime films that he had directed in the United States before enforced exile in Europe due to the Hollywood blacklist.

Rather than being seen as a template for the kind of cool 'masculinity in motion' that Melville's later films exemplify, *Du rififi chez les hommes* seems rather to be a film more exactly positioned on the cusp of social change. It is certainly conservative in terms of its treatment of women as either figures of spectacle, duplicity or preoccupied maternity – it is noticeable, for instance, how Jo's wife *is* actually shown repeatedly cleaning the flat with her recently acquired vacuum cleaner – but its conception of male interrelationships is arguably more concerned to show the inherent flaws behind such active homosociality. These are, in fact, hardly men that 'get it right'. The film appears to posit the idea that despite the initial success of the raid on the part of the 'gangster family', there is also a melancholic degree of futility in their efforts. It wants to show the virtues of loyal male cooperation, but it also demonstrates the consequences of betrayal. In this sense, the film is as pessimistic about men in themselves as it appears to be about the interaction between men and women. The question mark lingering over the picture of the young Tonio at the end of *Du rififi chez les hommes* is in the order of what kind of man he will grow up to be: one like his namesake? In this sense, Dassin is clearly suggesting that a female-centred home might actually be a safe place.

Why this emphasis on social as well as criminal failure? As I have already mentioned, it is tempting to see *Du rififi chez les hommes* and its counterpart *Touchez pas au grisbi*, as Robin Buss and others have done, as covert war films in that their narrative drives of 'comradeship'[18] and betrayal allowed the fault lines of the French Resistance to become displaced onto a more permissible form of representation – that of the milieu of the Parisian gangster. It is certainly worth remembering that Tony's rivals, the Grutters, have an explicitly German-sounding name and noting that the fastidious efforts to unlock the safe resemble some kind of undercover raid. This idea is convincing in that it is plausible to believe, as Susan Hayward has noted,[19] that French filmgoers were not yet ready to see more ambivalent and less codified treatments of their recent past.[20] However, it is also possible to suggest that the director of *Du rififi chez les hommes* had a more personal investment in showing the virtues of working-class domesticity. As a socially aware director with intense left-wing credentials, Dassin wanted at least to show Jo's motivation for turning to crime in the first place: the very 'American' desire for a better life for himself and his son. In this sense, *Du rififi chez les hommes* is as much a film looking backwards to the liberal social documentarist impulses of such films as *The Naked City* as forwards to the emotional but depoliticized suspense of future heist films like Melville's *Le Deuxième souffle* (1962) and *Le Cercle rouge* (1970).

Dassin was also, as we already know, a recent victim of the anti-communist hearings in the United States and, as such, was acutely aware of the legacy of what happens when political elements that encourage people to speak out against each other poison that most cooperative of enterprises – filmmaking. His picturing of the personal devastation wrought by a group of men whose endeavours fall apart from betrayal and the failure to see things through, may also in this sense have less to do with a fear of the female sphere than with a recognition of the kind of hurt that he had himself recently experienced.

We can explore these ideas in more detail by turning to two exemplary moments in the film. The first is the dialogue-free sequence detailing the four men's departure for the heist. This begins with a dissolve from Tony sealing the ringing dummy alarm with fire extinguisher foam in the thieves' den to Louise standing over Tonio asleep in his bed. The aural and visual dissonance between the two spaces is striking. The first is harsh, mechanical and subversive; the second is ordered, domestic and natural. As Louise hears a sound off-screen she moves across to the bedroom doorway, shielding herself from the view of Jo, who enters screen right in the hallway to pick up his case and exit through the main entrance. Louise pauses then closes the bedroom door and Dassin holds this shot momentarily as if to describe simultaneously the painful fact of Jo's absence and Louise's decision to 'close off' the reality of what is about to unfurl. Doorways continue to function throughout the sequence. Each time they feature as a motif, they build towards a pattern that will be repeated in the play on internal and external space within the heist sequence itself. The difference here is that the emphasis is on what is being left behind rather than what is being infiltrated.

We cut to a view of Mario's galley kitchen with his girlfriend Ida in the foreground gathering the dishes and him resting on a bench distractedly handling a colander of the same circular shape as the many visual elements to come in the picturing of the raid. By now, we can begin to hear the plaintive off-screen humming of Viviane who is slowly reprising the 'Rififi' tune. This time, the heterosexual couple acknowledge each other – albeit without any conversation – and Mario touches Ida fondly on her breast with his finger. Unlike the female figure, who is only half-dressed and now relegated literally to doing the washing up, Mario is dressed to the hilt in his dandyish appropriation of the same male attire that featured so extensively in the dramatization of Viviane's previous version of the number. His appearance and the way it features actively within the *mise-en-scène* of the film as a whole, matches Stella Bruzzi's explanation that such costuming serves a clear homosocial function within the context of the French gangster film. 'The over-identification with appearance and the open display of fetishistic interest in each other's clothes,' she argues, 'has obvious homoerotic undertones, signifying a dual attraction for a man who[m] the gangster both desires and wants to become.'[21] Although

Jo's departure: doorways onto doorways

writing more specifically about the trappings of such characters as the one
Alain Delon played in *Le Samouraï*, her suggestion is that

> this simultaneous refraction and condensation of the image in the
> construction of an 'ideal ego' offers a productive way of extending the
> instabilities of the gangster beyond the American model. [Here], competition
> and emulation are clearly foregrounded towards the French gangster who is
> caught obsessively measuring his actual ego by the ego he himself has created
> from past cinematic images.

The conflation of the reprise of Viviane's number and the departure of
the over-dressed Mario thus serves a dual function. First, it reminds one
of the instability of the roles played by the male types in the film in order
to reiterate the counterfeit nature of their enterprise and ultimately their
relationships with each other. Then second, and perhaps most
interestingly in the context of this being a French film directed by an
American émigré, it points to the cultural cross-fertilization being
employed here to describe national and generic identification. To return
to Bruzzi again, Mario's and also César's subsequent costuming, along
with the performative aspect of Viviane's melody 'Rififi', clearly refer to
'the mutual scavenging, cross-referencing and straight copying ...
perpetrated since the French cinema of the 1950s began to express its
fondness for Americana.'[22] In short, these are men about to re-enact what
the song has already partly foretold.

  As if to underline this point, Dassin then moves to the actual nightclub where the source of the non-diegetic music is revealed and we see
Viviane rehearsing her number for that evening's performance. In an
extended long take, we watch her interact with her fellow musicians on
the floor of the club before the camera reveals César discretely gazing
from the wings screen left onto the action. The difference in the camera
setup here is revealing. The play on seeing and remaining unseen, which
permeated Jo and Mario's previous departures, is distorted in favour of a
more theatrical perspective suggested by the replacement of a doorway
with a set of curtains. We are thus encouraged both to share César's
voyeuristic gaze onto the action and to understand that the camera's
attention to the display of the song's reprise is indicating a portent of
things to come. Viviane's slow accentuated delivery of the tune may
sound like the calm before the storm, but if one imagines the structure of

the narrative portrayed in the way the song was previously delivered, it appears more as if she is somehow 'in the know'. She alone is aware of the trouble men bring to themselves.

The song does not continue. Instead, Dassin cuts to an image of a solitary Tony in his forlorn apartment with George Auric's melancholic string arrangement of the 'Rififi' tune now heard on the soundtrack. There is no woman in his life to say farewell to. This is the most 'French' of the four departures in that the *mise-en-scène* of the shot with its faded wallpaper, bare furnishings, gloomy lighting, bottle of wine and Ricard ashtray on the table evoke the memory of the doom-laden poetic realist boarding rooms inhabited by Jean Gabin in *Le Jour se lève* and Arletty in *Hôtel du nord* (Marcel Carné, 1938). Tony turns to the table, puts out his cigarette and then languidly exits through the final doorway of the sequence. His domestic milieu is a world away from the more 'Americanized' noir cityscape in which he then, as we have seen, immediately finds himself. In this sense, this is the most overt instance of crossover between two traditions of urban noir representation in the film.

Only later in the film do we see the significance of the four men

Mario's departure: a divided *mise-en-scène*

Tony's apartment: the legacy of poetic realism

setting off on their own terms. It shows that unlike the more enduring familial nature of the gangsters' realm in *Touchez pas au grisbi* where Max even spends the night with Riton, their mutually supportive relationship is provisional. This is especially evident in the sequence immediately after the raid when the men reveal their deeper motivation for undertaking the heist to each other. It takes place in Mario's apartment where he, César and Jo are waiting for Tony to arrive. The four men gather silently around a table and gaze intently at the covered jewels placed in the centre. They then exchange nervous looks in anticipation. Their eyes return to the table and Mario whips away the cloth covering the small sack containing the gems. With still no words being spoken, Jo moves the sack in front of Tony.

Tony pauses anxiously and then, just as he is about to draw the cord open, Dassin cuts away to a medium close-up of an expectant Mario gazing off-screen right. The next two shots of César, then Jo, are identical. The combined effect of this play on anticipation and seeing but not seeing (on the parts of the characters and the spectator) intensifies the suspense and revives the visualization of the men's collaboration in

The 'family' united for the final time

the heist. We still do not see the jewels. The camera tracks in to Tony's face and as he spills the bag's contents onto the table we only hear the sound of them chinking against each other. To reiterate the emotional force of the moment, Dassin returns to a succession of four individual close-ups of the men's faces (all sharing the same eyeline) before finally revealing the outcome of all the men's plans and work. This is the final sequence in the film when the 'family' of men appears to be so united in its purpose.

From hereon in, the group begins to dissolve. The turning point is when they discuss what the money will mean to them. For Mario, it means that he and Ida can try out the beds in all the most chic hotels. César will be able to 'purchase' husbands for his sisters. Jo only thinks of a better future for his son. The men turn to Tony and ask him what he wants. He has to pause and ask the question of himself aloud. With a deep sigh, he admits he has no idea. As we have seen before in the departure sequence, he has no other family to which to turn. Already, the outcome of the heist has produced a sense of futility that will only become amplified as the film's further tragic events unfurl.

A transnational film noir?

By the time Dassin had completed *Du rififi chez les hommes*, his critical holding in France was such that his first 'French' film was bound to attract considerable attention. As we have seen, a key element of Dassin's unique place as an émigré American director assigned to produce an adaptation of a French crime novel shot in Paris was his ability to meld together certain formal and social concerns displayed in his American noir work with a profound sensitivity towards the conventions of popular film genre in a European context. To what extent then can *Du rififi chez les hommes* actually be considered a transnational film noir?

Some answers to this question can be found by returning to the attitude of French writers towards Dassin's status and reputation as a leading director of Hollywood film noir. In their book on American noir cinema, Borde and Chaumeton specifically picked up on the way in which Dassin had previously defined his aesthetic principles to French readers of *Cahiers du cinéma*.[23] They noted his decision to highlight a preference for a 'mixture of documentary and poetry'.[24] 'Such a feeling for detail is only given to the great filmmakers,' they noted. 'Through it, dialogue, gestures and settings become meaningful.'[25] These aspects of Dassin's style, especially the emphasis on gesture and location, are precisely what made it so amenable to one strand of contemporary French realist cinema. The director's fusion of a detailed observational documentary aesthetic with a more lyrical aspect to the picturing of urban crime may initially remind one of the conventions of French poetic realism, but poetic realism had largely had its day by the late 1940s. Dassin (and Agostini's) evocative camerawork, with the odd exception, is really more reminiscent of the penetrating quotidian quality of some of the images in such late 'social noir' films as Julien Duvivier's bitter character study of Les Halles, *Voici le temps des assassins* (1956). To this extent, although *Rififi* shows none of the cynical unease underlying this work, Borde and Chaumeton may be said, in part, to be claiming Dassin as an honorary European.

The late 1940s and early 1950s were marked by a return to debates about the aesthetics of realism in general and a detailed evaluation of the work of the Italian neo-realists, especially Roberto Rosselini and Vittorio de Sica.[26] In the light of such concerns, for example, André Bazin had written approvingly of Dassin's preceding work on *The Naked City*. Dassin's interests as a filmmaker were at a different end of the noir spectrum from those of his American counterparts like Orson Welles or Anthony Mann (especially in his work with the cinematographer John Alton) who tended to favour a more embellished visual style laden with expressive shadows and dramatic camera angles. His treatment of Paris, for an outsider, is remarkably assured for its observation of the different levels of social class and, as we have also observed, sequences of *Du rififi chez les hommes* have a real feel for ordinary, as well as extraordinary, urban detail. These elements coincided with a resurgence of French street photography during the decade and their humanistic qualities were very likely partly to be what lay behind Dassin's success as an émigré director in France at the time. He came with the right credentials.

Although he may not initially have known it, Dassin was in many ways the right kind of American director to treat the adaptation of such an important French crime novel. French film noir never especially favoured either the kind of oneiric hallucinatory qualities of some dark American crime films (which appealed to the French Surrealists as far back as the 1920s[27]) or the existential despair of the lonely American gumshoe or disillusioned male Second World War veteran. The figure of Tony in *Du rififi chez les hommes* thus appears to be an interesting kind of hybrid. He seems, like Dassin perhaps, to be a man out of time, a man without the kind of secure domestic networks that inform the disposition of his other colleagues in the heist. Also, he had neither the means nor the desire to emulate the American gangster prototype in the way that Jean-Pierre Melville's archetypal figures Jeff Costello (Alain Delon) in *Le Samouraï* or Silien (Jean-Paul Belmondo) in *Le Doulos* would later appear to do. In moving through the doorway of his poetic realist apartment to the hubbub of the American style big city at night, he exemplifies the hybrid tensions of the film as a whole.

These tensions, as we have seen, are visible throughout the film. Dassin begins with a nod to the stylized smoke-filled loucheness of *The Asphalt Jungle* then moves immediately to a detailed consideration of the geography of the ordinary French city café. The heist undertaken by a Swede and Italian, as well as two Frenchmen, takes place in one of the most international parts of the French capital in a business owned by the British.

Much of the rest of the film is set in the cosmopolitan nightspots of Pigalle, where foreign visitors (and fellow criminals) are featured within the narration. A scene towards the end of the film even shows the young Tonio playing cowboys in the gardens of the Tuilleries. Sections of the film such as the funeral by the banks of the River Seine have an intimate but plaintive naturalism to them, while other parts seem to foreground a strong degree of narrative and stylistic self-consciousness, in fact to such an extent that spectators are encouraged to detach themselves from the diegesis and speculate on the meta-narrative potential of the song that refers to the film's very title. I have suggested that Viviane's song (and the elaborate means by which its performance is visualized) suggests a lack of substance. But we might also wish to think about the ways the film, as a whole, conveys at certain moments a porous sense of identity and lack of coherence regarding key aspects of its film style. As we now turn to discuss the critical reception of *Du rififi chez les hommes*, we shall continue to observe these issues within the wider context of Franco-American film relations of the period and see how Dassin's film continues to be a fascinating prism through which to observe some of the more fundamental faultlines of French cinema during the 1950s.

## Notes

1   See Ross, Kristin (1996) for a far more detailed discussion of the figure of the car as a key emblem of France's modernization in the 1950s and the analogous relationship that may be drawn, in this period, between the 'movement, image, mechanization, standardization' of the car and the phenomenology of speed contained within the moving image (pp. 19–21).
2   The window was an artificial construction. The sequence was actually shot on the street. See video interview with Jules Dassin on DVD release of *Du rififi chez les hommes* (Criterion Publishing, 2001).
3   Mappin & Webb was founded in 1774 by Jonathan Mappin and it remains one of the UK's leading retailers of fine jewellery and silverware. It is the silversmith to the royal family.
4   Tony's surname, le Stéphanois, implies he is from the St Etienne region of France. His 'Swedish' identity must surely be a reference to the part of 'Swede' that Burt Lancaster played in Robert Siodmak's *The Killers* (1946).
5   Ginette Vincendeau (2003) p. 110. The figure of Arsène Lupin has featured in the following French (and American) films: *Arsène Lupin* (Michel Carré, 1909); *Arsène Lupin contre Ganimard* (Michel Carré, 1914); *Arsene Lupin* (George Loane Tucker, 1916); *Arsene Lupin* (Paul Scardon, 1917); *Arsène Lupin* (Jack

Conway, 1932); *Arsène Lupin détective* (Henri-Diamant-Berger, 1937); *Arsène Lupin* (George Fitzmaurice, 1938); *Enter Arsene Lupin* (Ford Beebe, 1944); *Les Adventures d'Arsène Lupin* (Jacques Becker, 1957); *Signé Arsène Lupin* (Yves Robert, 1959); *Arsène Lupin contre Arsène Lupin* (Edouard Molinaro, 1962) and *Arsène Lupin* (Jean-Paul Salomé, 2004).

6 One may even suggest that, by the end of the film, the story has come full circle with the gang all dead and the money back in the hands of the authorities.

7 Something Jean-Pierre Melville reprised in *Le Doulos*. I owe this point to Ginette Vincendeau.

8 See, for example, *La photographie humaniste 1945–1968. Autour d'Izis, Boubat, Brassaï, Doisneau, Ronis ...* (Paris: Bibliothèque nationale de France, 2006); and Peter Hamilton, 'Representing the Social: France and Frenchness in Post-War Humanist Photography', in Stuart Hall (ed.) *Representation: Cultural Representations and Signifying Practices* (London: Sage Publications in association with the Open University, 1997) pp. 75–150.

9 For more on the femme fatale see Kaplan, E. Ann (ed.) *Women in Film Noir* (2nd edn) (London: British Film Institute, 1999).

10 For more on Abd el-Krim and the Rif republic, see Léon Gabrielli, *Abd el-Krim et les événements du Rif 1924–1926* (Casablanca: Editions Atlantide, 1953).

11 Edward Dimendberg (2004) p. 172.

12 Ibid., p. 172.

13 See Noël Burch and, Geneviève Sellier, *La drôle de guerre des sexes du cinéma français: (1930–1956)* (Paris: Natan, 1996).

14 Ginette Vincendeau, in Hughes and Williams (2001) p. 146.

15 Ibid., p. 146.

16 Ibid., p. 151.

17 Ibid., p. 153.

18 Robin Buss (2001) argues that Becker's film 'belongs to the same context as' *Du rififi chez les hommes* and Clouzot's *Le Salaire de la peur* (1953) pp. 41–2.

19 Susan Hayward (1993) p. 162.

20 In relation to this argument, see also the classic text on the legacy of the Occupation: Henry Rousso, *The Vichy Syndrome: History and Memory in France since 1944* (London: Harvard University Press, 1991).

21 Stella Bruzzi (1997) p. 75.

22 Ibid., p. 67.

23 François Truffaut and Claude Chabrol interviewed Dassin in the April 1955 (no. 46) pp. 3–13 and May 1955 (no. 47) pp. 11–16 issues of *Cahiers du cinéma*.

24 Borde and Chaumeton (1955) p. 171. Jacques Doniol-Valcroze also noted the relationship between 'lyricism' and 'realism' in the film. See *Cahiers du cinema*, April 1955 (no. 46), pp. 44–6.

25 Ibid.

26 Two of the classic texts here are André Bazin's 'An Aesthetic of Reality: Neo Realism (Cinematic Realism and the Italian School of the Liberation)', originally published in *Esprit* January 1948 and republished in André Bazin, *What is Cinema?* vol. II (Berkeley: University of California Press, 2005) pp. 61–78; and 'De Sica: Metteur en Scène', originally published in Italian in 1953 by Edizione Guanda, Parma and republished in André Bazin, *What is*

*Cinema?* vol. II (Berkeley: University of California Press, 2005) pp. 61–78. See also Jacques Rivette, 'Lettre sur Rossellini', *Cahiers du cinema*, no. 46, April 1955, pp. 14–26.

27    In his useful introduction to the English language translation of Borde and Chaumeton, James Naremore reminds us that Marcel Duhamel specifically reminisced about the Surrealists' fondness for American crime films in his own preface for the original book. See Raymond Borde and Etienne Chaumeton, *A Panorama of American Film Noir 1941–1953* (San Francisco: City Lights, 2002) p. x.

# 3 Reviewing *Rififi*

## A surprise success

By spring 1955 commercial expectations for *Du rififi chez les hommes* were running high. The release of a number of French crime films on the domestic and overseas markets marked the first anniversary of Jacques Becker's *Touchez pas au grisbi*. In anticipation of this, an article publicizing the resurgence of the French thriller in the winter issue of *Unifrance-Film* contained a glossary of French slang terms.[1] Production reports were published in the trade press on the other major Auguste Le Breton adaptation of the season, *Razzia sur la chnouf*, which had started shooting on 29 November 1954.[2] On 2 March *Série Noire*, directed by Pierre Foucard and starring Robert Hossein, was released. It took 19,793,880 francs in its first week.[3] *Razzia sur la chnouf* was released one week before *Du rififi chez les hommes* on 7 April and took 16,138,120 francs in receipts.[4] To coincide with Jules Dassin's first French film, *Cahiers du cinéma* published an extensive two-part interview (by François Truffaut and Claude Chabrol) in its April and May issues, thus firmly establishing the émigré director's status among the other great Hollywood auteurs of the *Cahiers* pantheon such as Howard Hawks, Nicholas Ray and Fritz Lang.

Yet it was by no means certain how successful the film would actually be. Dassin was still relatively unknown outside *cinéphile* circles and, as we have already seen, unlike *Razzia sur la chnouf*, which was marketed as a Jean Gabin vehicle, the film had no star names to publicize it. Only the brand of Auguste Le Breton provided a certain measure of the film's pedigree. Very soon though, it was obvious that the producers had a hit on their hands. The film took a considerable 28,315,520 francs in its first week nationwide and was seen by 83,275 spectators during this time.[5] By the middle of June in Paris, 302,691 tickets had been sold and the film had earned 98,286,970 francs.[6] Figures across France were even more extraordinary. Total earnings by 15 June were put at 199,457,871 francs and Pathé estimated that about 600,000 tickets had by then been sold throughout the country.[7] The film ended up coming ninth in box-office returns for all French films produced in 1954.[8] It was fortunate for Dassin that he had agreed to a percentage of the box-office income to compensate for the relatively minor amount he had originally been paid as his main salary. What undoubtedly helped the film's fortunes was its enormous success at the 1955 Cannes Film Festival. It was nominated for the Palme d'or and Dassin eventually jointly won the best director prize.[9] The Americans were reportedly furious that the French, rather than the American, flag went up at the awards ceremony. But how, considering the circumstances, could it be otherwise?

By the mid-1950s, the number of French films being exported across the Atlantic was rising[10] and *Du rififi chez les hommes* also went on to do well in Dassin's home country. At the time of its screening in Cannes, *Variety*'s international correspondent, Gene Moskowitz, gave the film an approving review. 'This looks like the peak of the gangster pic series here,' he told his American readers.

> Until now, this cycle has been an imitation of America's best. This pic, however, is something intrinsically Gallic without sacrificing the rugged storytelling. For the US, chances are more highly problematical since it lacks star names. Editing is first-rate as is Philippe Agostini's lensing. This is Dassin's first pic in five years and shows he has not lost his touch.[11]

In line with Moskowitz's predictions, when the film was released on 5 June 1956, it was initially not exhibited outside the limited art-house cinema circuit in a number of major cities. It ran for 20 weeks, for example, in a single cinema in Manhattan.[12] Writing in the *New York Times*, Bosley Crowther thought that the film made 'the characters in Mickey Spillane seem like sissies'. *Du rififi chez les hommes* was 'the keenest crime film that ever came from France but there is also a poetry about it'. It had 'a flavor of crooks and kept women and Montmartre "boites" that you can just about smell'.[13] As a measure of its expected market, the film was initially only distributed in subtitled prints, but it was later released again in a dubbed version retitled *Rififi Means Trouble!* The Roman Catholic Legion of Decency objected to aspects of the film's treatment of violence and sexuality and awarded it a 'C' ('condemned') rating. But, as Lenny Borger points out, commercial expediency intervened and 'after three brief cuts and the addition of an opening title card consisting of a quote from the Book of Proverbs (5), [the film] was upgraded to the "B" category (morally objectionable in part for all).'[14] The aptly chosen proverb read: 'When the wicked are multiplied, crime shall be multiplied: but the just shall see their downfall.'[15]

British critics felt similarly compelled to inform their readers of the meaning of 'rififi'. On the whole, they were more equivocal and their opinions pointed to a number of rather stereotypical conceptions of popular French and American culture. Most praised the visual quality of the film's heist sequence. Gavin Lambert, writing in the *Sunday Times*, was typical in his assertion that the 'film's narrative technique … accumulates excitement in a series of quick, bold, assertive strokes.'[16] On the other hand, many also thought that the narrative significance of the robbery, along with the ensuing brutality of betrayal and retribution, was disappointing. C. A. Lejeune wrote, for example, that she found the depiction of the crime 'lucid but morally regrettable'.[17] Like many reviewers who saw an analogous relationship with the then critically despised American crime film, Lejeune argued that 'At its clumsiest "Rififi" is just another vulgar piece of violence, no more edifying because the scene is Montmartre and the players (headed by Jean Servais) are French than if the cast had been picked in Hollywood and the scene were Chicago or New York.'[18] Derek Granger concurred, pointing to 'the film's rather ordinary limitations. … Why ever should "hoodlums" seem suddenly chic and philosophical to boot because they happen to be speaking in the accents of Pigalle rather than Brooklyn?' he asked.

> The answer, of course, is that they don't; and though we may note a few physical differences which set them apart from their better-fed transatlantic counterparts – these French ne'er do wells are altogether a weedier and more

haggard lot – such characteristics are doubtless the result of too many Gauloises and an excess of black coffee.[19]


## 'A film without indulgence'

There is no doubt that *Du rififi chez les hommes* was marketed and received as a French film although there is evidence that the French were acutely aware from the outset that its director was an American émigré working in France for the first time. In the press publicity for the film at the Cannes Film Festival, for example, it was specifically announced, as if to counteract any pre-existing anxieties about the film being chosen as part of the 'French Selection', that Jules Dassin had 'been surrounded by an *entirely French* [my italics] first-rank team'.[20] The critic in *Les Nouvelles littéraires* was scathing that an American had been chosen to represent France at the nation's premier international film festival. This only served, in his opinion, to underline the way in which the French film industry was currently pandering to the lowest common commercial denominator by seeking to emulate 'the violence and eroticism' of American crime cinema. 'Because imitation makes perfect, the producers of *Rififi* have decided to hire an American director', he argued. Only the excellence of the heist sequence, told 'with the precision of a documentarist, distinguished [it] from hundred of other [such films] coming from his home country'.[21]

Others were more generous. Most agreed that the film was an advance on the source novel that *had* been written by a native Frenchman. François Truffaut wrote, for instance, that 'Jules Dassin has made the best "noir" film I have ever seen from the worst *roman noir* I have ever read.'[22] Louis Chavet, writing in *Le Figaro*, praised the director's flexibility. 'Jules Dassin ... has easily adapted his style and technique to the character of the people and places of our country,' he stated. 'He knows how to depict the secret fauna of Paris with a lively veracity that most of our own filmmakers have neither previously been capable of or concerned with.' In short, 'Jules Dassin subtly makes a certain French tradition of psychological realism his own.'[23] Jean-Paul Marquet, writing later in the monthly film journal *Positif*, agreed and made the important distinction that the director had made a virtue of the fact that he did not know France as well as a native filmmaker.

He noted how some had talked of the film's treatment of the French capital in terms of 'a Paris à l'américaine'. But, as he went on to argue, Dassin's eye was really more like that of a visiting provincial. *Du rififi chez les hommes*, in fact, contained 'the kind of poetic images that only an outsider, rather than a local, can observe.'[24]

For the most part then, the French press actually received *Du rififi chez les hommes* very positively. What specific elements of the film were singled out for critical attention? First, there was the virtuoso treatment of the representation of the central act of crime. Nearly all reviews paid attention to the decision to film the heist sequence without any dialogue or music although, as we have already seen in our analysis of the text, several were wrong to suggest that the robbery was 'silent'. Indeed, it is also interesting to observe how many critics were so immersed in the process of the robbery that their estimates of the amount of screen time it took ranged significantly from ten to thirty minutes. Jean-Paul Faure (one of the more accurate reviewers in this regard), writing in *Paris-presse*, suggested that 'this near silent half an hour will feature as a highlight in future film anthologies.' It is 'a recital in real cinema'. The key to the success of the sequence for many critics lay in its detailed, almost forensic, immersion in the detail on the part of the protagonists, and the corresponding feelings of psychological tension that this induced on the part of the spectator. 'Dassin forces every spectator to live each dramatic moment with the same intensity as the film's heroes,' Faure wrote. 'He makes the public participate.'[25] Interestingly, Jean-Paul Marquet explicitly contrasted this sense of phenomenological engagement with the representation of crime in Clouzot's *Les Diaboliques*. Here, the decision not to reveal the mystery of the headmaster's 'death', and make that the very modus operandi of the narrative suspense felt on the part of the spectator, was seen as analogous to the trickery specifically deployed within the film's diegesis. 'When one compares [Dassin's treatment of the robbery] to the dishonest – there's no other word – proceedings in *Les Diaboliques*,' he wrote, 'the simplicity and delicacy of Dassin borders on the miraculous.'[26]

The second recurring element many French critics signalled was the quality of the performances in the film and here again issues of national identity mattered. Having noted the American nationality of the film's director, critics often turned to the ways in which the skill of the French actors, especially Jean Servais, contributed to the film's underlying 'authenticity'. This approval served two functions. First, it allowed the lack of any leading French star figures in *Du rififi chez les hommes* to be compensated by the reassuring guarantee of the display of native acting prowess. Second, it helped to seal an illusion of realism and veracity to the film's depiction of the Parisian underworld, which, as we shall see, then became a central discursive element of the film's politics and assumed moral position. To give an indication of the strength of this strand of the film's critical reception, the most important crime novelist in French culture at the time, Georges Simenon, was quoted at Cannes saying that Dassin's film was 'fantastic'. 'I didn't know actors of such intensity and simplicity as Jean Servais existed in France. For me, this is of great interest in relation to my own characters!'[27]

A number of commentators also noticed that the film's American director had cast himself as an Italian character in his first French film. In a second illuminating review of *Du rififi chez les hommes*, Truffaut went further by arguing that there was actually an interesting duality between Dassin's qualities as a director and the personality of the character he played in his own production. He observed an analogous relationship between the exemplary fastidiousness and skill of César and the kinds of specialists in the activities of daily life that populated the films of John Ford and even the novels of Balzac. This, in turn, led him to speculate on the overall 'sublimely Pirandello-like' quality of *Du rififi chez les hommes* in which the skills of the thieves paralleled the craft of the filmmaking. Thus, he argued somewhat rhetorically, 'Thanks to his extraordinary talent, Jules Dassin has managed, over the course of twenty-eight minutes, to convince us of the moral and professional value, even social usefulness of these partners-in-crime.'[28]

The third aspect of the critical response to the film, as we have already begun to see, was the emphasis on the lyrical documentary aspects of its *mise-en-scène*, especially in relation to the representation of Paris. A number of critics noticed the distinctive way in which Dassin and his cinematographer, Philippe Agostini, pictured the French capital. Writing in *Libération*, Simone Dubreuilh interestingly compared the film's atmospheric treatment of Paris with the way that Carol Reed and Robert Krasker had vividly photographed the backstreets of postwar Vienna in

*The Third Man* (1949). Central to this was a sense of revelation based on the outsider perspective of the film's director. *Du rififi chez les hommes*, she argued, portrayed 'the disturbing and poetic side of the city captured by those who know how to breathe, listen, watch, wait, look out and above all stroll ... in other words love the genuine face of the city unnoticed by official tourist guides.'[29] Dubreuilh also related aspects of the film's distinctive style to the observational aesthetics of European city documentarists such as Walter Ruttman, Joris Ivens and Georges Franju. 'The rigour of the images [in the film], their austerity, the authenticity of the gestures, moments of hesitation and the sounds is striking', she argued. François Truffaut agreed. 'The surest value of the film rests in the tone of the work. ... The relative liberalism of French censorship has allowed Dassin to make a film without indulgence, immoral perhaps but nonetheless profoundly noble, tragic, warm-hearted and human.'[30]

## The politics of realism

This question of the film's 'tone' was central to the realism that formed a crucial aspect of the discursive history of *Du rififi chez les hommes*. There were two main strands to this. First, there was the matter of the recurring association drawn between Dassin's filmmaking style and recent trends in European cinema. We have already seen how some French critics previously saw a connection between Dassin's committed social conscience and the means by which his camera chose to focus on the ordinary details of human life in American films like *The Naked City*. This continued when the director arrived in France with the result that *Du rififi chez les hommes* was generally seen less in terms of a break in Dassin's career than one might have expected. In the pressbook Unifrance prepared for the film, for example, it was explicitly stated that 'Jules Dassin is one of the pioneers of what is known as neo-realism.'[31] This emphasis on continuity rather than rupture also neatly allowed Europeans to claim the film's director as one of their own. He might well have been seen as a political fish out of water in the current political climate of the United States, but this meant that in Europe he was specifically welcomed for his apparent ability to see the world as it was.

Furthermore, Dassin was also seen as capable of reinvigorating a popular cinematic genre that had begun to seem tired and out of touch. Gilles Martain was typical in the way he observed this dialogue between the fictional and the real in the film. What was new compared with earlier efforts in the genre, he pointed out, was the 'exactitude' with which 'the landscapes, streets or even atmosphere'[32] of the streets of Paris were realized. Martain, like other writers who sought to isolate the aesthetic distinctiveness of Italian neo-realism, emphasized the blurring of boundaries in the Parisian location sequences of *Du rififi chez les hommes*. 'It is difficult to make out the difference between the actors and the passers-by caught within the camera's field of vision,' he argued. In one telling phrase, summing up this veneration for the film's distinctive quotidian realism, he suggested that Dassin 'knows exactly how to implant fiction onto reality, like a brightly coloured image on a wall.'[33]

Crucially, as noted in the previous chapter, this degree of urban realism was of a different order than poetic realism. Martain thought that there were 'admirable shots of Paris' in the film but, in fact, they 'ignore[d] the romanticism of Carné'.[34] For many critics, the 'strikingly evocative power'[35] of these shots lay rather in their sociological immediacy as if the real could somehow coexist on screen along with the contrived and fictional. For the first time then in the French film noir, it was as if the spectator was really there. In other words, part of this complicity between the image and the spectator rested absolutely in a coherent sense of fidelity. If one could first recognize the world of the film, then one could also simultaneously believe in the extraordinary events that occurred within its spectacular diegesis.

This reworking of generic convention mattered to a second strand of criticism that concerned the film's much noted *psychological* realism. In an important article published in *Radio cinéma télévision*, André Bazin went further than other critics in trying to situate *Du rififi chez les hommes* in relation to the legacy of poetic realism, especially in terms of its impact on the development of French noir cinema. Bazin saw the 'noir realism' of the prewar period as a hybrid form, which 'stemming from the naturalist tradition of [Jacques] Feyder and [Jean] Renoir secretly married this national tendency with an expressionism derived from German and Nordic cinema. [Jacques] Prévert then added,' in his opinion, 'a touch of surrealism to the mix'.[36] For Bazin, 'The darkness in these films was such that it held the depth and mystery of the night, not to mention the universe, with ease.'[37] What mattered to a number of critics, but especially Bazin, was the way in which more recent noir films had displaced this tradition by an emphasis on material surface rather than emotional profundity. In place of 'the depth and mystery of the night, most current French [noir] films are nothing more than recipes, or even mere dustjackets!'[38] he wrote. What made *Du rififi chez les hommes* and its other favoured counterpart, *Touchez pas au grisbi*, more successful was their renewed attention to the urban everyday and a specific ability to rework (rather than directly imitate) that characteristic melding of décor and psychology found in the French cinema of the 1930s.

Jean de Baroncelli concurred. He saw Dassin's film (like Becker's) as more than just a crime film. It 'shines with a particular brilliance amongst the floodtide of film noirs with which we are currently being submerged', he wrote. For de Baroncelli, the secret was that Dassin had not 'abandoned his characters. He [had not] turned them into robotic objects of abjection. *Rififi* isn't only a gangster film. It's also a film about comrades.'[39] This is what Bazin was referring to in a second article on *Du rififi chez les hommes* in which he argued that film genre always had to mean more than redundant repetition. Here, he specifically criticized the ambiguous psychological authenticity claimed by Auguste Le Breton who saw his own form of realism in the exact correlation between his personal experiences of the criminal world in Paris and the use of slang in his fiction. Good noir cinema had to do more than that for Bazin since 'A system based [just] on convention always ends up by becoming worn out.'[40] Jean-Paul Marquet agreed with this idea by arguing that the distinctiveness of Dassin's film lay in its very refusal to observe 'all the inherent tendencies of the genre' in relation to characterization. Not only was the film interested in the psychology of male comradeship, but its strength also lay in the decision to refute 'the sacrosanct "law of the underworld", that Corneille-like conflict found at the level of the "*série noire*" as a whole'.[41] A key instance of this radical break with custom could be seen in the anguished aftermath of the robbery when Tony conducts his brutal but principled punishment murder of César amid the theatrical backdrops of the L'Age d'Or nightclub.

Various political tensions emerged in this discussion of the film's interest in social documentation and psychology and, again, they go back to the critical history of French film noir in the 1930s. Earlier on, we observed that when the term 'noir' emerged in French critical discourse during that decade, it was initially a pejorative one signalling either a degree of impurity (on the right) or moral disgust (on the left). Communist critics such as Georges Sadoul continued to see postwar noir in these terms and this affected their distinctive reception of *Du rififi chez les hommes*. Although it would be unwise to consider that the left-wing press was especially influential on the general filmgoer, it is nonetheless interesting to observe the cultural reception of Dassin's film given the important political factors that initiated his arrival as an émigré filmmaker in France. Georges Sadoul, in particular, was contemptuous of the now firmly established genre of Série Noire film adaptations. Writing in *L'Humanité*, he argued that 'The "Série Noire film" seems to have become for most directors no more than an exercise in style,' although he did go on to note that 'I'd rather believe that it is more a purely commercial constraint which leads to a waste of talent.'[42] What especially seemed to arouse Sadoul's ire was the imitative aspect of the Série Noire phenomenon in that it was relying on the same issues informing its American film noir counterpart: first, a conviction in the commercial exploitation of seriality and repetition regarding film form and narrative and then, second, a belief in the righteousness of capitalism in telling moral stories about the societies it was responsible for negatively shaping. Thus, he suggested that the Série Noire was being 'sold by the gross like tins of corned beef with their standardized seasonings'.[43] He went on to argue that since 'Every regime has the mythology it deserves ... the heroes of "the free world" remain gangsters and their Olympus can be found in the underworld. If the gangster film comes to us from the United States, the mecca of capitalism, then that isn't by chance.'[44] To sum up, there was therefore a porous boundary between commercial opportunity and the very subject of representation. Only Dassin's status as a left-wing émigré came as a form of saving grace and Sadoul keenly articulated the injustice of his (and others such as John Berry's) forced exile from the United States. At least in this sense *Du rififi chez les hommes*, unlike its predecessor *Razzia sur la chnouf*, had some form of moral core. 'The underworld for Dassin is like

Dante's hell: you have to abandon all hope as you enter,'[45] he finally countered.

For some, this apparent evacuation of overall moral responsibility for the treatment of crime in the film carried its own implications. Jean-Paul Marquet reported that during the aftermath of a screening at the Musée Guimet in Paris, the majority of the audience complained that the supposed immorality of the film had repulsed them. At a provincial screening, the chaplain of a secondary school and the local representative of the Communist Party were apparently similarly united in their disapproval.[46] It was left to others to discern the underlying morality of *Du rififi chez les hommes*. Marquet pointed out that the film, in fact, was especially ethical in the way it revealed the 'emptiness'[47] of the characters' desires. And Dassin spoke out about these concerns. At a post-screening discussion organized by the FFCC (Fédération Française des Ciné-Clubs), he made the point – hitherto unnoticed by all the critics – that the young figure of Tonio could in fact be seen as the real moral core of the film. Quoting a phrase uttered by Pierre Grutter in the film, he reminded his audience that the boy's own 'future [was] sombre'. 'At the age of 5 years old, one already has eyes and ears,' he argued.[48]

Sadoul was not alone in referring to the mythical aspects of the French film noir. In what may partly be seen as a riposte to much of what has been said above, André Bazin articulated a firm but reasoned synthesis of some of these critical positions. It is worth quoting at length. Bazin's starting point was an article by H. F. Rey in *France-Observateur* that had been published the previous week. In it, Rey had apparently assembled the views of a number of real gangsters on the recent spate of Série Noire films within France. This, in turn, led Bazin to speculate about the profound set of relations between fiction and reality and between cinematic genre and aesthetic innovation. 'Like the novel but even more so, the crime film is essentially mythical,' he argued.

> Whether it's a matter of *Scarface*, Maigret, Lemmie Caution or the heroes of *Grisbi*, the success of the crime thriller genre is only comprehensible in terms of a mythology, fundamentally modern and urban, which is the fruit of big city civilization and its mechanistic totalitarianism.

He went on to say that

It is nonetheless true however that reality *can* [my italics] serve it: by either the renewing of themes that the unfurling of history proposes to the novelist or filmmaker, or by a documentary exactitude which supports the myth, reinforces its credibility and maintains a useful confusion between reality and that which it is a substitute for.[49]

It was this very 'confusion' that he saw at the root of the aesthetic, moral and political brilliance of *Du rififi chez les hommes*. The film 'offers us a perfect example of the dialectic between realism and myth in the crime thriller genre,' he thought. It was important to stress that 'the profound nature of the film is [indeed] aesthetic. The issue for its characters is *not* [my italics] psychological realism, but tragic necessity and nothing would be more absurd to wonder if the character of Jean Servais expressed the mentality of the underworld badly or well.' In his analysis, unlike some of the film's less subtle critics, Bazin therefore *did* distinguish between reality and the imposition of 'a documentary rigour' on the text itself. To conclude, for him, 'Dassin's film would have lost all its interior symmetry and its fine aesthetic economy if it had been composed entirely either in the style of the robbery or in the style of the death of le Stéphanois.'

## Audiences, trade and culture

The politicization of postwar French film culture forms an important context for *Du rififi chez les hommes* since it allows us to explore further the unique significance of the film in relation to the dialectical nature of Franco-American cultural relations during this period. As an American émigré in Europe, Jules Dassin was clearly the victim of an unpleasant and, to many liberal French, morally repugnant political regime in the United States. His previous work as a director of film noir within the Hollywood system had demonstrated that he was already, in part, a natural outsider. Politically motivated support within the French film industry for 'L'Affaire Dassin' had similarly demonstrated this when left-wing professionals campaigned on his behalf to give him leave to work in France after his forced exile from Hollywood. Given these concerns and the ambivalent attitude towards the United States they revealed, it was no accident that film noir in general swiftly became *the* Hollywood genre that allowed the

French to venerate the achievements of its practitioners while also recognizing the social and political corruption at the heart of its representation of American society. But as we shall now see, its European counterpart, the French noir crime thriller, also became a privileged site from which to observe cultural tensions between the two countries, especially where they concerned discourses within the French film trade and the formation of its changing audiences.

The initial response to the spate of American films, including several seminal film noirs, when they flooded French screens at the end of Occupation was mixed. Edgar Morin thought that France needed 'the American cinema like an old friend back from afar,'[50] while the director Julien Duvivier, returning from his own exile in Hollywood, argued that 'If we let ourselves be invaded by American production without a countervailing place for French films, in two years there will be no more French cinema.'[51] The key mechanism for dealing with this particular issue and for subsequently safeguarding the developmental interests of the French film industry *vis-à-vis* Hollywood was the signing of the Blum–Byrnes accords in Washington on 28 May 1946. This led to the imposition of a quota of French films to be screened in every French cinema.[52] Historians now agree that the agreement gave the French film industry the breathing space it needed to recuperate from the war since 'the quota of French films allowed to be shown roughly reflected the potential production capacity of the French film industry at the time.'[53] At the time, however, the political response was adverse. Many demonstrators such as Jacques Becker, Simone Signoret and Louis Daquin – the same people who later took to the streets in support of Jules Dassin – protested vigorously under the auspices of the Institut des Hautes Études Cinématographiques (IDHEC), the Communist Party and the Confédération Générale du Travail (CGT). This, in turn, led to the formation of the influential Centre National de la Cinématographie (CNC)[54] on 26 October 1946. The CNC campaigned for the first *Loi d'aide* in August 1948, which provided a raft of further measures to shore up the fortunes of the French film industry.[55] The passing of the *Loi d'aide* coincided with a revised Blum–Byrnes agreement (known as 'the Paris agreement'), which extended the quota of French films and introduced further restrictions on the number of American films to be shown on French screens. But, by now, the economic arguments for protectionism were less compelling than the cultural ones and the remaining years up to the release of *Du rififi chez les hommes* in 1955 were therefore largely dominated by a number of related developments that had an impact on the reception of Dassin's film.

The 1950s were in fact boom years for the French film industry with the total number of spectators going to the cinema outclassing the previous heyday of the 1930s. As Richard Kuisel points out, during the decade 'the French were [actually] able to maintain about half of their box office and to limit Hollywood's share to a third.'[56] By the middle of the 1950s, at the time of the release of *Du rififi chez les hommes*, 'French films [were earning] 50 per cent of total receipts with only 30 per cent of the movies in circulation.'[57] As Jean-Pierre Jeancolas remarks, just the following year, in 1956, out of a total of 399 million domestic spectators, the proportion of those going to see French films as opposed to American ones was 48.6 per cent to 33.4 per cent.[58] What these figures suggest is that, by the middle of the decade, the likelihood of any mainstream French film by an established Hollywood director attracting negative opprobrium had declined dramatically compared with just ten years previously. What mattered more was the film's actual take on French society and, as we have seen, Dassin was the perfect figure to articulate a hybrid response to the resurgence in the popularity of the French crime film.

A further important aspect of this was, in part, due to measures taken during the changes in postwar film legislation. One outcome of the second *Loi d'aide* passed in August 1953, for example, was investment in the FFCC and the Cinémathèque Française, then under the aegis of Henri Langlois. This, in turn, helped assure the development of a new metropolitan and cine-literate audience that prior to the advent of the Nouvelle Vague also formed an important and lasting constituency for crossover films like *Du rififi chez les hommes*. The decade of the 1950s saw the proliferation of cinéphilia in France and Dassin's film particularly benefited from the shift in audience demographics that this entailed.[59] This era, for instance, marked the key moment in the French exodus from the rural regions to the cities, especially Paris, which impacted on the formation of taste and the critical evaluation of modernity and popular culture in two important ways. First, as Vincendeau has pointed out, 'although Paris and large cities gained an enormous amount of people, at the same time, another movement within these cities ... was pushing them towards the suburbs – a cultural environment which did not promote cinema attendance.'[60] The suburbs *were*, in fact, still screening films – television had not quite displaced the cinema by 1955[61] – but these nonetheless tended to be second-run features that had been in circulation for some time. Pierre Sorlin estimates, for example, that in the year of the release of *Du rififi chez les hommes* there were as many as 3500 films in overall circulation in France, but only 380 of these were actually first-run titles being shown in city centres; the rest were two to three years old and were being shown on local neighbourhood screens in the tradition of 'le cinéma du samedi soir'.[62] This shift of middle-brow cinema away from the city centre contributed to a powerful critical backlash against the ordinary tastes of the middle market – increasingly characterized as backward looking, staid and conservative.[63] Thus, we begin to see the emergence of a new cultural sphere that specifically venerated the sorts of films from which the middle market was, in part, being denied access – a certain kind of Hollywood cinema that could be celebrated for its style, vigour and, above all, alternative outlook on modern life.

As Vincendeau rightly points out though, there *was* an exception to the rule that 'the desire to serve a specific middle-class *cinéphile*, and increasingly international audience meant ... [a distancing] from a cinema that addressed a popular French audience through narrative, stylistic, and referential patterns with roots in indigenous French culture.'[64] This was the thriller. For this reason, Dassin's film thus became *the* perfect hybrid text. *Du rififi chez les hommes* not only revealed evidence of distinctive aesthetic cross-fertilization: it was a French film noir shot by an important Hollywood émigré, but it also demonstrated that it was capable of simultaneously addressing both a popular and a *cinéphile* audience to equal critical and commercial acclaim.

Dassin, in a way, was but the latest in a long line of dissident Americans welcomed by the French and rendered acceptable to audiences through their accommodation to popular taste. Figures like Sidney Bechet and Josephine Baker were just a few of many African American musicians and singers who forged long lasting careers on the other side of the Atlantic during the interwar years.[65] Having said this, one should not give the impression that all Americans in Paris met with universal acclaim and all forms of transatlantic American popular culture were equally accepted during the postwar years. Vincendeau has pointed out, for instance, that broadly speaking the French embrace of American popular culture tended to take two distinctive forms: the 'original' and the 'dubbed'.[66] These aspects were dependent on class. In the first instance, the middle-classes or members of the urban cultural intelligentsia largely favoured the 'original'. The exchange between the Left-Bank bohemia of Saint-Germain and American jazz artists like Miles Davies and Duke Ellington was an example of this. In the second, one saw more assimilation or reconfiguration, for example in the way the colloquialisms of the American actor Eddie Constantine were successfully deployed in popular crime cinema.[67] Again, Dassin's work in France seemed to straddle the divide. His status as a Hollywood auteur and as a cultural figure capable of profound cultural adaptation assured this. On the one hand, his status among the cinéphiles assured a degree of continuity. The French critical response to his American work indeed embodied all the contradictory tensions at the heart of the cinéphilic response to Hollywood with regard to popular French film. Like others such as Vincente Minnelli and John Ford, he was praised for the craftsmanship of his *mise-en-scène* and his productive engagement with mainstream genre cinema, but these were the same factors that counted so negatively against his French counterparts of the time. On the other hand, *Du rififi chez les hommes* showed that Dassin had benefited enormously from a creative dialogue with French technicians like Philippe Agostini and French actors like Jean Servais, in fact so much so that it is equally possible to argue that the film represented a new direction in the career of this most cosmopolitan figure. In other words, the film can finally be seen as a vital turning point not just in its director's life, but in terms of it being an unlikely but nonetheless successful location for the condensation of a number of significant cultural trends.

## Notes

1  Jill Forbes, in Rigby and Hewitt (1991) p. 97.
2  *Le Film Français*, 19 November 1954, page unknown.
3  *Le Film Français*, 18 March 1955, page unknown.
4  *Le Film Français* 22 April 1955, p. 27.

5   *Le Film Français*, 6 May 1955, p. 35.
6   IDHEC file on *Du rififi chez les hommes* (Bifi library, Paris).
7   Production and Distribution file CN1042 B546 (Bifi library, Paris).
8   Siclier and Levy (1986) p. 21.
9   With Sergei Vasilyev for *Geroite na Shipka/Shipka Heroes* (1955). *Du rififi chez les hommes* also later won the critics award for best film of 1956 from the SFCC (Le Syndicat Français de la Critique de Cinéma).
10  Steve Lipkin, in Hanlin (1986) p. 171.
11  *Variety*, 15 June 1955, page unknown.
12  The Fine Arts Theater, 128 E. 58th Street. See Lenny Borger: www.filmforum.org/archivedfilms/rififipress.html (accessed 30 December 2006).
13  *New York Times*, 6 June 1956, page unknown.
14  Ibid.
15  Further release dates for the film were Denmark (10 June 1955); Japan (21 September 1955); West Germany (30 September 1955); Sweden (21 November 1955); Finland (17 April 1959). See http://www.imdb.com/title/tt0048021/releaseinfo (accessed 1 July 2006).
16  *Sunday Times*, 3 July 1955, page unknown.
17  *The Observer*, 3 July 1955, page unknown.
18  Ibid.
19  *Financial Times*, 4 July, page unknown.
20  *Le Film Français*, Special Spring Issue nos. 567–8, p. 17.
21  *Nouvelles littéraires*, 21 April 1953, page unknown.
22  *Arts*, 20 April 1955, page unknown.
23  *Le Figaro*, 14 April 1955, page unknown.
24  *Positif*, no.14–15 (November 1955) p. 71.
25  *Paris-presse*, 19 April 1955, page unknown.
26  *Positif*, nos 14–15 (November 1955) p. 72.
27  *L'Aurore*, 30 April 1955, page unknown.
28  *Arts*, 18 May 1955, page unknown.
29  *Libération*, 19 April 1955, page unknown.
30  *Arts*, 20 April 1955, page unknown.
31  Pressbook for *Du rififi chez les hommes*, BFI National Film Library (microfiche).
32  *Rivarol*, 22 April 1955, page unknown.
33  Ibid.
34  Ibid.
35  Ibid.
36  *Radio cinéma television*, 24 April 1955, page unknown.
37  Ibid.
38  Ibid.
39  *Le Monde*, 14 April 1955, page unknown.
40  *France-Observateur*, 29 April 1955, page unknown.
41  *Positif*, no.14–15 (November 1955) p. 72.
42  *L'Humanité*, 20 April 1955, page unknown.
43  *Lettres Françaises*, 22 April 1955, page unknown.
44  *L'Humanité*, 20 April 1955, page unknown.
45  Ibid.
46  *Positif*, no.14–15 (November 1955) p. 73.
47  Ibid.

48  Ibid.
49  *France-Observateur*, 29 April 1955, page unknown.
50  Quoted in Jean-Pierre Jeancolas (1998) p. 48.
51  Quoted in Jean-Pierre Jeancolas (1998) p. 49.
52  From 1 July 1946, for two years, every French cinema was required to show a French film for a minimum of four weeks over a three-month period. See Jean-Pierre Jeancolas (1991) p. 65.
53  Ginette Vincendeau (1992) p. 58.
54  The CNC developed from the Comité d'Organisation des Industries Cinématographiques (COIC) that had been established in 1940.
55  They included the development of a support fund to subsidise the distribution and exhibition of French and French language dubbed features. This was financed by the establishment of a *taxe spéciale additionnelle* (TSA) based on ticket sales at the box-office. See Jean-Pierre Jeancolas (1991) p. 64.
56  Richard Kuisel (2000) p. 120.
57  Ibid., p. 121.
58  This compared with figures of 387 million spectators and a ratio of 42.4 per cent to 44.5 per cent in 1949. See Jean-Pierre Jeancolas (1998) p. 53.
59  For more on the history of cinéphilia in France, see Christian Keathley, *Cinephilia and History, or The Wind in the Trees* (Bloomington: Indiana University Press, 2006) and Antoine de Baeque, *La Cinéphilie: invention d'un regard, histoire d'une culture, 1944–1968* (Paris: Fayard, 2003).
60  Ginette Vincendeau (1992) p. 60.
61  There were just over 125,000 television sets in French homes in 1955, which represented about 1 per cent of the population. Frédéric Gimello-Mesplomb (2006) p. 141.
62  Pierre Sorlin (1991) pp. 74–5.
63  The classic article here would be François Truffaut's 'Une certaine tendance du cinéma français', *Cahiers du cinema*, no. 31 (January 1954) pp. 15–29.
64  Ibid., p. 64.
65  See, for example, Tyler Stoval, *Paris Noir: African Americans in the City of Light* (Boston: Mariner Books, 1998) and William A. Shack Berkeley, *Harlem in Montmartre: A Paris Jazz Story Between the Great Wars* (Los Angeles: University of California Press, 2001).
66  Ginette Vincendeau (1992) p. 62.
67  Ibid., p. 79.

# 4   Reviving *Rififi*

## After *Du rififi chez les hommes*

Jules Dassin lived with both the achievement of *Du rififi chez les hommes* and the disappointment of his professional exile from the United States for the rest of his working life. It was a turning point in his career in a number of ways. He never worked in Hollywood again.

In the year following the release of the film and its triumph at the Cannes Film Festival, it was distributed around the world to great success. The story goes that *Du rififi chez les hommes* was so influential – in the wrong sense of the word – that in Mexico the authorities had to withdraw it 11 weeks into its Mexico City run because of an uncontrollable spate of similar robberies.[1] On the back of the film's commercial acclaim, Dassin was offered work on the screen adaptation of Nikos Kazantzakis's *Christ Recrucified*. The script of *Celui qui doit mourir* (1957) – a retelling of the Gospels set in 1920s' Greece – was co-written by his fellow blacklisted North American émigré Ben Barzman, and the film reunited several of the cast from *Du rififi chez les homes*, including Jean Servais and Carl Möhner. Like its director's first French film, it was also produced by Henri Bérard, scored by Georges Auric and edited by Roger Dwyre. It also featured his future wife Melina Mercouri, whom he had met at Cannes. For much of his subsequent life, he remained in Europe living as an American citizen in Greece.

A measure of the remaining animosity Hollywood's commercial

establishment felt towards Dassin was revealed the subsequent time he attended Cannes to mark the festival screening of *Celui qui doit mourir*. Dassin's account has it that since the film was again accorded the status of a French film and since both he and Barzman were both still seen as *persona non grata* in Hollywood, they were originally excluded from an important cultural reception at the US embassy. Eventually, the authorities relented but, much to the amusement of the French press, which covered the event, the majority of their fellow American guests snubbed the pair visibly. Only Gene Kelly made a point of taking Dassin by the arm and leading him up the steps in defiance.[2]

Dassin went on to work on many successful and popular European productions. Along with *Du rififi chez les hommes* and his early American film noirs he is probably best remembered today for his two most commercially successful Melina Mercouri features – *Never on a Sunday* (1960), the lighthearted romantic comedy telling the story of an affair between a local Greek prostitute and a visiting American classical scholar aptly named Homer, and *Topkapi*, the comedy caper film set in Istanbul that revisited the world of international jewellery thieves. The latter, shot in colour, was the antithesis of *Du rififi chez les hommes* in terms of the vibrant palette of its cinematography and the sly, humorous tone of its story. The robbery sequence at the Topkapi Palace, however, is still remarkably suspenseful.

Was the blacklist a blessing in disguise for Dassin? He often claimed in interviews that he valued the degree of artistic freedom from which he benefited in his later European work, but in truth, as he also remarked, he remained separated from his roots. 'I was separated from my cultural background, and I had to improvise and pretend to understand other cultures well. ... The blacklist was a horrible, monstrous idea – attacking a man in his most vulnerable, vital need,' he commented.[3] It is telling that Dassin never renounced his American citizenship.

*Du rififi chez les hommes* was also good to Auguste Le Breton. Today, the prolific crime writer is largely remembered for being the author of the novel that formed the basis of the film. Le Breton, as we have already noted, also worked on another heist film – Jean-Pierre Melville's *Bob le flambeur*. If Dassin's film was an impersonation of a French film by an American, Melville's concerns the impersonation of an American character by a Frenchman. Some of the film's atmospheric detailing of Paris by cinematographer Henri Decaë, aspects of its wry character observation (especially concerning the psychology of male loyalties), as well as its elegiac interest in the figure of an ageing gangster patriarch, all appear to point to Dassin's film, but *Bob le flambeur* really shows little of its precursor's intrinsic interest in the art of robbery. Indeed, the heist is never actually seen to take place; we only witness the elaborate rehearsal for the event. Overall, Melville's film feels more like a semi-improvised sketch than Dassin's more polished, classical drama. In this sense, it looks forward to the early films of the Nouvelle Vague rather than backwards to the established conventions of the 'tradition of quality'.[4]

Le Breton continued writing and, as already mentioned, a number of his published memoirs revitalized his own notorious self-mythology that permanently associated him with the denizens of the French underworld. Just as Dassin increasingly became an international figure, so the Rififi sequence itself began to travel. The author created a dozen works that retained the name 'Rififi' and linked it to such glamorous countries as Argentina, Cambodia and Hong Kong (see Appendix 5). Many of Le Breton's other books were also adapted for the screen, including *Le Rouge est mis* – another tale of crime and betrayal – shot by Gilles Grangier in 1956 and starring Jean Gabin, Lino Ventura and Annie Girardot (see Appendix 3).

## Influences

It is notoriously difficult to ascertain the 'influence' of a particular piece of work and we must remember that Dassin would always specifically deny any association between *Du rififi chez les hommes* and what now appears to be its most immediate predecessor, *The Asphalt Jungle*. It is easier to point out the enduring sense that his film represented a kind of template for making the model heist film. With this in mind, one must acknowledge the dialogue in which Melville's *Le Cercle rouge* seems to engage with *Du rififi chez les hommes*, not least because we know that its director at one time entertained the notion of directing the adaptation of Le Breton's novel himself rather than using an American. *Le Cercle rouge* is an extraordinary film. It shares some of its predecessor's attributes, not least a powerful degree of investment in the close examination of the male visage and an almost pathological interest in the attainment of mute perfection regarding the enactment of crime. But it is also a very different work. The France (and Paris) it occupies is a world away from the relatively cosy and familial networks of Dassin and Becker's films. To observe this, one has only to compare the treatment of the two nightclub sequences. In contrast to the rather convivial, old-fashioned glamour of the L'Age d'Or, the club in *Le Cercle rouge* is distinctively colder, more heartless and anonymous. The geographical range of the two films is different too and this lends an almost operatic melancholy to the muted colour of the wintry landscapes that form an important element in the opening sections of Melville's work. The aesthetic sphere of postwar French humanist photography seems long gone; a brooding sense of ordered modernity has replaced it. The immersion in the heist is similarly detailed and gripping, but even the space in this sequence is more extended. Rather than relying on a vertical plane of action in which the thieves operate in the room above the loot, for example, the geography is more horizontal and linear, thus losing some of the dialectic between seen/unseen and inside/outside noted previously.

Major heist films to which one can link *Du rififi chez les hommes* include, among many, *The Killing* (Stanley Kubrick, 1956); *Odds Against Tomorrow* (Robert Wise, 1959); *Ocean's Eleven* (Lewis Milestone, 1960) and its remake by Steven Soderburgh in 2001; *Mélodie en sous-sol* (Henri Verneuil, 1963); *Le Clan des Siciliens* (Henri Verneuil, 1969); *The Italian Job* (Peter Collinson, 1969); *Thief* (Michael Mann, 1981); *Reservoir Dogs* (Quentin Tarantino, 1992); *The Usual Suspects* (Bryan Singer, 1995); *Snatch* (Guy Ritchie, 2000); *Heist* (David Mamet, 2001) and *Inside Man* (Spike Lee, 2006). There are also correspondences between Dassin's attentive cinema of process and the observational aesthetics at work in two other important French films of the 1950s, both of which concerned the portrayal of men seeking to escape from the confines of prison: Robert Bresson's *Un condamné à mort s'est échappé* (1956) and Jacques Becker's final film, *Le Trou* (1959), again based on a Série Noire novel but this time by José Giovanni.

Less serious was Mario Monicello's hilarious parodic take on *Du rififi chez les hommes*, *I Soliti ignoti* (1958), which reprised the basic narrative thrust of the original but set the heist among a group of washed-up thieves and unemployed men in the working-class suburbs of Rome. The characterization of the four main protagonists largely followed the patterning of Dassin's film and the timing of their exchanges and banter is exemplary. Visually, the film marries a distinctive neo-realist aesthetic with some distinctive night-time visuals, but the tone of the film is relentlessly satirical to the point where the audience is constantly left waiting for the next miscalculation or pratfall on the part of the hapless criminals. Rather than successfully making away with the loot, for example, they drill into the wrong wall and cause the apartment to flood. In a fitting twist to the intercultural history of *Du rififi chez les hommes*, Monicello's film was remade as *Crackers* by the Frenchman Louis Malle in San Francisco in 1984.

## The *rififi* brand

Given the memorable rhythm of the phrase, 'Rififi', and its potential almost to become a kind of shorthand for a form of crime drama set in the gangster underworld, it is not surprising that the term has proliferated in the years after the release of *Du rififi chez les hommes*. As well as the 'Rififi Around the World' series of books of which a couple were filmed – *Du rififi à Tokyo* (Jacques Deray, 1960) and *Du rififi à Paname* (Denys de la Pattelière, 1966) – there was also a sequel of sorts, *Du rififi chez les femmes*, which Alex Joffé adapted for the screen in 1959. The film had nothing very much to do with the original apart from the similarity of the title, the fact that Robert Hossein again featured among the cast and the inclusion of another heist, this time of the Bank of Belgium. It also starred Eddie Constantine, Pierre Blanchar and Françoise Rosay. The term 'Rififi' was widely used elsewhere in European cinema. In 1967, Howard Morris's caper comedy, *Who's Minding the Mint*, became known as *Rififi à la Americana* in Spain. In Germany, the groundbreaking British gangster film, *The Long Good Friday* (John Mackenzie, 1980), was retitled *Rififi am Karfreitag*.

'Rififi' has even entered the general culture. When a gang of British jewel thieves stole £30,000 worth of jewellery from a shop in Newbury in

1979, using the same techniques that featured in the film, the police immediately nicknamed them 'The Rififi Gang'.[5] In keeping with the times, 'Rififi' now has a more ironic, postmodern set of associations largely to do with its retro-cool image of the criminal highlife. There are various Rififi clubs in parts of the UK and USA. One can, for example, visit the Rififi Club and Restaurant in the heart of London's Mayfair where such dishes as 'Mobster Thermidor' feature on the menu. Further north in Manchester, one can also find 'ambience, tranquillity and atmosphere' at the Rififi Nightclub.[6] There's a similar venue in New York.

## Rififi returns

And now *Du rififi chez les hommes* is about to be remade. Its director will again be American but this time it will be shot entirely in the USA. The new version of the film ties in with Hollywood's recent spate of vintage crime film remakes that began with Neil Jordan's restyling of *Bob le flambeur*, *The Good Thief* (2002). It has continued with *The Italian Job* (F. Gary Gray, 2003) and the success of the franchise that has, so far, seen *Ocean's Eleven* (2001), *Ocean's Twelve* (2004) and *Ocean's Thirteen* (2007). Strictly speaking, there has already been a remake of sorts: Ralph Nelson's *Once a Thief* (1965) which borrows significant plot elements from Dassin's film, but retells the narrative from the point of view of Jo. Here, Jo was renamed Eddie Padek, a San Francisco ex-con who agrees to take part in one last heist organized by his racketeering brother played by Jack Palance. The Franco-American connections were numerous. Jacques Bar produced the film for MGM and it even starred the French actor, Alain Delon, in the leading role.

The new adaptation of Le Breton's book will simply be called *Rififi* and Harold Becker is slated to be the film's director. It will star Al Pacino in the role originally played by Jean Servais. Pacino is certainly of the age now to be a convincingly world-weary gangster, but will there be replacements for the many other wonderful supporting actors who populated the original? And what about Paris – in some ways, the film's greatest unacknowledged character? At least, as I hope we have seen in the course of this book, the status of the original is now assured as a truly classic crime film from the heyday of French popular genre cinema. To conclude, *Du rififi chez les hommes* will always have the allure, suspense and dramatic feel of what François Guérif has so eloquently termed 'a Greek tragedy shot in Pigalle.'[7]

## Notes

1  See video interview with Jules Dassin on DVD release of *Du rififi chez les hommes* (Criterion Publishing, 2001).
2  Ibid.
3  Dassin interviewed in McGilligan and Buhle (1997) p. 223.
4  The 'tradition of quality' was a term Jean-Pierre Barrot coined in the weekly film magazine, *L'Écran français*, to describe the tradition of the well-made middle-market French film that filmmakers like Jean Delannoy and Christian-Jaque made. It later famously became the target of François Truffaut's polemical attention.
5  *Daily Mail*, 21 May 1979.
6  See http://www.rififi.co.uk/ (accessed 20 September 2006).
7  François Guérif (1981), p. 26.

# Appendix 1: Credits
## *Du rififi chez les hommes* (1955)

Indusfilms, Prima Film, Société Nouvelle Pathé Cinéma
1: 37: 1
115 minutes
35mm
Date of first screening: 13 April 1955 (Paris)

Director: Jules Dassin
Producer: René Gaston Vuattoux
Associate producers: Henri Bérard, René Bezard, Pierre Cabaud
Screenwriters: Jules Dassin, René Wheeler, Auguste Le Breton
Cinematographer: Philippe Agostini
Editor: Roger Dwyre
Production designers: Alexandre Trauner; Auguste Capelier
Music composer: Georges Auric
Song 'Le Rififi': Jacques Larue (lyrics) M. Philippe-Gérard (music)
Conductor: Jacques Métehen
Dresser: Henriette Ridard
Dress designer: Rosine Delamare (with Marcelle Desvignes)
Make-up artist: Anatole Paris
Make-up assistant: Marcelle Testart
Interior decorator: Roger Fresca
Camera operator: Jean-Marie Maillols
Production supervisor: Wilhelmine Berard
Unit manager Jean Goiran; Louis Mannella
Assistant directors: Patrice Dally, Bernard Deflandre, Jean-Jacques Vierne
Assistant editor: Denise de Casabianca, Nadine Trintignant (as Nadine Marquand)
Assistant camera: André Domage (as André Domage Lemoigne), Chenglesy
Assistant designers: Robert André, Gabriel Paris
Sound recordists: Charles Akerman, Jacques Lebreton, Jean Philippe
Location managers: Georges Kougoucheff, Pierre Charron
Props managers: Maurice Terrasse, Charpeaux
Continuity: Renée Nitzschke
Stills photographer: Begue
Jewelry provided by Dusausoy
Furs: Renel

CAST

Jean Servais (Tony le Stéphanois)
Carl Möhner (Jo le Suedois)
Robert Manuel (Mario Ferrati)
Jules Dassin (as Perlo Vita) (César le Milanais)
Marie Sabouret (Mado)
Janine Darcey (Louise)
Claude Sylvain (Ida Ferrati)
Marcel Lupovici (Pierre Grutter)
Robert Hossein (Rémi Grutter)
Pierre Grasset (Louis Grutter)
Magali Noël (Viviane)
Dominique Maurin (Tonio)
André Dalibert (as Dalibert) (Webb, le bijoutier)
Marcel Lesieur (as Lesieur) (Fredo)
Fernand Sardou (First gambler)
Armandel (Second Gambler)
Jacques Besnard (Third gambler)
Teddy Bilis (Teddy Laurentin)
Alain Bouvette (Footman, 'L'Age D'Or')
Émile Genevois (Charlie)
Marcelle Hainia (Fredo's wife)
René Hell (Un camelot)
Daniel Mendaille (Lookout)
Marcel Rouzé (First gendarme)
Maryse Paillet (Charlie's mother)
Roger Rudel (French voice of Jo le Suédois)
Jacques David (unaccredited)
Jenny Doria (unaccredited)
Alice Garan (unaccredited)
Huguette Montreal (unaccredited)
Gilbert Moreau (unaccredited)
Lita Reccio (unaccredited)

# Appendix 2: Jules Dassin filmography

1941    *The Tell-Tale Heart*
1942    *Nazi Agent* (a.k.a. *Salute to Courage*)
        *Reunion in France* (a.k.a. *Mademoiselle France* and *Reunion*)
        *The Affairs of Martha* (a.k.a. *Once Upon a Thursday*)
1943    *Young Ideas*
1944    *The Canterville Ghost*
1946    *A Letter for Evie*
        *Two Smart People*
1947    *Brute Force*
1948    *The Naked City*
1949    *Thieves' Highway* (a.k.a. *The Thieves' Market* and *Collision*)
1950    *Night and the City*
1955    *Du rififi chez les hommes* (a.k.a. *Rififi*)
1957    *Celui qui doit mourir* (a.k.a. *He Who Must Die* and *Colui che deve morire*)
1959    *La Legge* (a.k.a. *The Law* and *Where the Hot Wind Blows*)
1960    *Pote tin Kyriaki* (a.k.a. *Never on Sunday*)
1962    *Phaedra* (a.k.a. *Faidra*)
1964    *Topkapi*
1966    *10:30 P.M. Summer*
1968    *Up Tight!*
        *Hamilchama al hashalom* (a.k.a. *Survival 1967* and *Comme un éclair*)
1970    *Promise at Dawn* (a.k.a. *La Promesse de l'aube*)
1974    *The Rehearsal* (a.k.a. *I Dokimi*)
1978    *A Dream of Passion* (a.k.a. *Kravyi yinekon*)
1980    *Circle of Two* (a.k.a. *Obsession*)

# Appendix 3: Auguste Le Breton filmography

## Screen adaptations of books by Auguste Le Breton

1955   *Razzia sur la chnouf* (Henri Decoin)
       Screenplay: Henri Decoin, Maurice Griffe, Auguste Le Breton
       (Le Breton also makes brief appearance as himself)
       *Du rififi chez les hommes* (Jules Dassin)
       Screenplay: Jules Dassin, René Wheeler, Auguste Le Breton
1956   *Le Rouge est mis* (Gilles Grangier)
       Screenplay: Michel Audiard, Gilles Grangier, Auguste Le Breton
       *La Loi des rues* (Ralph Habib)
       Screenplay: Ralph Habib, Jean Ferry
1957   *Rafles sur la ville* (Pierre Chenal)
       Screenplay: Paul Andréota, Pierre Chenal, Jean Ferry
1959   *Du rififi chez les femmes* (Alex Joffé)
       Screenplay: Alex Joffé, José Giovanni, Gabriel Arout, Jacques Mage
1962   *Du rififi à Tokyo* (Jacques Deray)
       Screenplay: José Giovanni, Rodolphe-Maurice Arlaud, Jacques Deray
1964   *Sokaklarin kanunu* (Aram Gülyüz) (English title: *Law of the Streets*)
       Screenplay: Aram Gülyüz
1966   *Du rififi à Paname* (Denys de la Pattelière)
       Screenplay: Alphonse Boudard, Denys de La Patellière, Franco Dal Cer
       (Italian dialogue)
       Brigade antigangs (Bernard Borderie)
       Screenplay: Bernard Borderie, Francis Cosne, Auguste Le Breton
1969   *Le Clan des Siciliens* (Henri Verneuil)
       Screenplay: Henri Verneuil, José Giovanni, Pierre Pelegri
2007   *Les Hauts murs* (Christian Faure)
       Screenplay: Albert Algoud

## Original screenplays by Auguste Le Breton

1956   *Bob le flambeur* (Jean Pierre Melville)
       Screenplay: Auguste Le Breton, Jean Pierre Melville
       (remade as *The Good Thief* by Neil Jordan, 2002)

# Appendix 4: Cited films

*27 Rue de la Paix* (Richard Pottier, 1937)
*À bout de souffle* (Jean-Luc Godard, 1960)
*Angèle* (Marcel Pagnol, 1934)
*Ascenseur pour l'échafaud* (Louis Malle, 1958)
*Bob le flambeur* (Jean-Pierre Melville, 1955)
*Boomerang!* (Elia Kazan, 1947)
*Brigade antigangs* (Bernard Borderie, 1966)
*Carrefour* (Curtis Bernhardt, 1938)
*Casbah* (John Berry, 1948)
*Ça va barder* (John Berry, 1954)
*Cécile est morte* (Maurice Tourneur, 1944)
*Cet homme est dangereux* (Jean Sacha, 1953)
*Coup de torchon* (Bertrand Tavernier, 1981)
*Crackers* (Louis Malle, 1984)
*Crossfire* (Edward Dmytryk, 1947)
*Descente aux enfers* (Francis Girod, 1986)
*Double Indemnity* (Billy Wilder, 1944)
*Drôle de drame* (Marcel Carné, 1937)
*Du rififi chez les femmes* (Alex Joffé, 1959)
*Entrée des artistes* (Marc Allégret, 1938)
*Fanfan la Tulipe* (Christian-Jaque, 1952)
*Fantômas* (Louis Feuillade, 1913–14)
*Gilda* (Charles Vidor, 1946)
*Heist* (David Mamet, 2001)
*Hôtel du nord* (Marcel Carné, 1938)
*House on 92nd Street* (Henry Hathaway, 1945)
*I Soliti ignoti* (Mario Monicelli, 1958)
*Inside Man* (Spike Lee, 2006)
*Je suis un sentimental* (John Berry, 1955)
*Jeunesse* (Georges Lacombe, 1934)
*Jour de Fête* (Jacques Tati, 1948)
*Kiss Me Deadly* (Robert Aldrich, 1955)
*Kiss of Death* (Henry Hathaway, 1947)
*La Bête humaine* (Jean Renoir, 1938)
*Ladri di biciclette* (Vittorio De Sica, 1948)
*La Lune dans le caniveau* (Jean-Jacques Beinix, 1983)
*La Môme vert-de-gris* (Bernard Borderie, 1953)
*La Tradition de minuit* (Roger Richebé, 1939)
*Laura* (Otto Preminger, 1944)

*Le Casse* (Henri Verneuil, 1971)
*Le Cercle rouge* (Jean-Pierre Melville, 1970)
*Le Clan des Siciliens* (Henri Verneuil, 1969)
*Le Crime de Monsieur Lange* (Jean Renoir, 1936)
*Le Dernier tournant* (Pierre Chenal, 1939)
*Le Deuxième souffle* (Jean-Pierre Melville, 1962)
*Le Drame de Shanghaï* (G. W. Pabst, 1939)
*L'Ennemi public no. 1* (Henri Verneuil, 1953)
*L'Étrange M. Victor* (Jean Grémillon, 1938)
*Le Jour se lève* (Marcel Carné, 1939)
*Le Mystère de la chambre jaune* (Henri Aisner, 1949)
*Le Petit monde de Don Camillo* (Julien Duvivier, 1952)
*Le Plaisir* (Max Ophuls, 1952)
*Le Puritain* (Jeff Musso, 1937)
*Le Quai des brumes* (Marcel Carné, 1937)
*Le Rouge est mis* (Gilles Grangier, 1956)
*Le Samouraï* (Jean-Pierre Melville, 1967)
*Les Enfants du paradis* (Marcel Carné, 1945)
*Les Diaboliques* (Henri Georges Clouzot, 1955)
*Les Disparus de Saint-Agil* (Christian-Jaque, 1938)
*Les Femmes s'en balancent* (Bernard Borderie, 1954)
*Les Loups chassent la nuit* (Bernard Borderie, 1952)
*Les Misérables* (Raymond Bernard,1933)
*Les Portes de la nuit* (Marcel Carné, 1946)
*Les Trois mousquetaires* (André Hunebelle, 1953)
*Le Témoin de minuit* (Dimitri Kirsanoff, 1953)
*Le Trou* (Jacques Becker, 1959)
*Leur dernière nuit* (Georges Lacombe, 1953)
*Mademoiselle Docteur* (G. W. Pabst, 1937)
*Massacre en dentelles* (André Hunebelle, 1951)
*Méfiez-vous des blondes* (André Hunebelle, 1950)
*Mélodie en sous-sol* (Henri Verneuil, 1963)
*Minuit… Quai de Bercy* (Christian Stengel, 1953)
*Mission à Tanger* (André Hunebelle, 1949)
*Mr And Mrs Smith* (Alfred Hitchcock, 1941)
*Murder, My Sweet* (Edward Dmytryk, 1944)
*Ocean's Eleven* (Lewis Milestone, 1960)
*Odds Against Tomorrow* (Robert Wise, 1959)
*Once a Thief* (Ralph Nelson, 1965)
*On Dangerous Ground* (Nicholas Ray, 1952)
*Orphée* (Jean Cocteau, 1949)
*Panic in the Streets* (Elia Kazan, 1950)
*Pépé le moko* (Julien Duvivier, 1937)
*Processo contra ignoto* (Guido Brignone, 1952)
*Quai des Orfèvres* (Henri Georges Clouzot, 1947)
*Quartier sans soleil* (Dimitri Kirsanoff, 1939)
*Razzia sur la chnouf* (Henri Decoin, 1955)
*Remorques* (Jean Grémillon, 1941)

*Reservoir Dogs* (Quentin Tarentino, 1992)
*Roman Holiday* (William Wyler, 1953)
*Rue barbare* (Gilles Béhat, 1984)
*Série noire* (Alain Corneau, 1979)
*Si Versailles m'était conté* (Sacha Guitry, 1954)
*Snatch* (Guy Ritchie, 2000)
*The Asphalt Jungle* (John Huston, 1950)
*The Big Heat* (Fritz Lang, 1953)
*The Good Thief* (Neil Jordan, 2002)
*The Italian Job* (Peter Collinson, 1969)
*The Killers* (Robert Siodmak, 1946)
*The Killing* (Stanley Kubrick, 1956)
*The Lavender Hill Mob* (Charles Crichton, 1951)
*The Long Good Friday* (John Mackenzie, 1980)
*The Public Enemy* (William Wellman, 1931)
*The Street With No Name* (William Keighley, 1948)
*The Third Man* (Carol Reed, 1949)
*The Usual Suspects* (Bryan Singer, 1995)
*They Drive By Night* (Raoul Walsh, 1940)
*They Knew What They Wanted* (Garson Kanin, 1940)
*Thief* (Michael Mann, 1981)
*This Gun For Hire* (Frank Tuttle, 1942)
*Thunder Road* (Arthur Ripley, 1958)
*Tirez sur le pianiste* (François Truffaut, 1960)
*Touchez pas au grisbi* (Jacques Becker, 1954)
*Une si jolie petite plage* (Yves Allégret, 1949)
*Un flic* (Maurice de Canonge, 1947)
*Un condamné à mort s'est échappé* (Robert Bresson, 1956)
*Un Linceul n'a pas de poches* (Jean-Pierre Mocky, 1974)
*Voici le temps des assassins* (Julien Duvivier, 1956)
*Who's Minding the Mint?* (Howard Morris, 1967)

# Appendix 5: 'Rififi à travers le monde'

## The 'Rififi à travers le monde' series of books

# Appendix 6: Select bibliography

Becker, Jens Peter, 'The Mean Streets of Europe: The Influence of the American "hard-boiled school" on European Detective Fiction', in C. W. E. Bigsby (ed.) *Superculture: American Popular Culture and Europe* (London: Paul Elek, 1975) pp. 152–9.

Borde, Raymond and Etienne Chaumeton, *Panorama du film noir américain 1941–1953* (Paris: Éditions de Minuit, 1955).

Bruzzi, Stella, *Undressing Cinema* (London: Routledge, 1997).

Buhle, Paul and Dave Wagner, *Blacklisted: The Film Lover's Guide to the Hollywood blacklist* (Basingstoke, Palgrave Macmillan, 2003).

Buhle, Paul and Dave Wagner, *Hide in Plain Sight: The Hollywood Blacklistees in Film and Television, 1950–2002* (Basingstoke: Palgrave Macmillan, 2003).

Buss, Robin, *French Film Noir* (London: Marion Boyars, 2001).

Cauliez, Armand-Jean, *Le Film criminel et le film policier* (Paris: Les Éditions du cerf, 1956).

Ceplair, Larry and Steven Englund, *The Inquisition in Hollywood: Politics in the Film Community, 1930–1960* (Berkeley: University of California Press, 1983).

Chartier, Jean-Pierre, 'Americans are also Making Noir Films', in A. Silver and J. Ursini (eds) *Film Noir Reader, 2* (New York: Limelight Editions, 1999) pp. 21–4.

Cieutat, Michel, 'Trois exilés du maccarthysme en Europe: Berry, Losey, Dassin', *CinémAction*, no. 56 (1990) pp. 109–13.

Crisp, Colin, *The Classic French Cinema 1930–1960* (Bloomington: Indiana University Press and London: I.B.Tauris, 1993).

Dimendberg, Edward, *Film Noir and the Spaces of Modernity* (Cambridge, Massachusetts: Harvard University Press, 2004).

Forbes, Jill, 'The "Série Noire"', in B. Rigby and N. Hewitt (eds) *France and the Mass Media* (London: Macmillan, 1991) pp. 85–97.

Forbes, Jill, *The Cinema in France: After the New Wave* (Basingstoke: Macmillan, 1992).

Frank, Nino, 'A New Kind of Police Drama: The Criminal Adventure', in A. Silver and J. Ursini (eds) *Film Noir Reader, 2* (New York: Limelight Editions, 1999) pp. 15–20.

Georgakas, Dan, 'The Way They Really Were', *Cinéaste*, vol. 23, no. 2 (1997) pp. 28–31.

Georgakas, Dan and Petros Anastasopoulos, '"A Dream of Passion" An Interview with Jules Dassin', *Cinéaste*, vol. 9, no. 1 (1978) pp. 20–4.

Gimello-Mesplomb, Frédéric, 'The Economy of 1950s French Cinema', *Studies in French Cinema*, vol. 6, no. 2 (2006) pp. 141–50.

Gorrara, Claire, *The Roman Noir in Post-War French Culture: Dark Fictions* (Oxford: Oxford University Press, 2003).

Grantham, Bill, 'Some Big Bourgeois Brothel': Contexts for France's Culture Wars with Hollywood (Luton: University of Luton Press, 2000).

Guérif, François, Le Cinéma policier français (Paris: Henri Veyrier, 1981).

Guicharnaud, Jacques, 'Of Grisbi, Chnouf and Rififi', Yale French Studies, 17, pp. 6–13.

Hayes, Graham 'Rififi', in P. Powrie (ed.) The Cinema of France (London: Wallflower Press, 2006) pp. 71–80.

Hayward, Susan, French National Cinema (London: Routledge, 1993).

Horton, Andrew, 'Jules Dassin: A Multi-National Filmmaker Considered', Film Criticism, vol. 8, no. 3 (1984) pp. 21–35.

Jeancolas, Jean-Pierre, 'The Setting-up of a "Method of Production" in the French Cinema of 1946–1950', in B. Rigby and N. Hewitt (eds) France and the Mass Media (London: Macmillan, 1991) pp. 59–67.

Jeancolas, Jean-Pierre, 'From the Blum–Byrnes Agreement to the GATT Affair', in G. Nowell-Smith and S. Ricci (eds) Hollywood and Europe: Economics, Culture, National Identity 1945–95 (London: British Film Institute, 1998) pp. 47–60.

Jeancolas, Jean-Pierre, 'The Reconstruction of French Cinema', in E. Ezra and S. Harris (eds) France in Focus: Film and National Identity (Oxford: Berg, 2000) pp. 13–21.

Kuisel, Richard F., Seducing the French: The Dilemma of Americanization (Berkeley and Los Angeles: University of California Press, 1993).

Kuisel, Richard F., 'The Fernandel Factor: The Rivalry Between the French and American Cinema in the 1950s', Yale French Studies, 98 (2000) pp. 119–34.

Le Breton, Auguste, Du rififi chez les hommes (Paris: Gallimard, 1953).

Le Breton, Auguste, Monsieur Rififi (Paris: Hachette, 1981).

Lipkin, Steve, 'The New Wave and the Post-War Film Economy', in B. Hanlin (ed.) Current Research in Film: Audiences, Economics and Law, vol. 2 (Norwood, New Jersey: Ablex Publishing Corporation, 1986).

McGilligan, Patrick and Paul Buhle, Tender Comrades: A Backstory of the Hollywood Blacklist (New York: St Martin's Press, 1997).

McArthur, Colin, Underworld USA (London: Secker and Warburg in association with the British Film Institute, 1972).

Naremore, James, More Than Night: Film Noir in its Contexts (Berkeley and Los Angeles: University of California Press, 1998).

O'Brien, Charles, 'Film Noir in France: Before the Liberation', Iris, 21 (1996) pp. 7–20.

Phillips, Alastair (2004) City of Darkness, City of Light: Émigré Filmmakers in Paris 1929–1939 (Amsterdam: Amsterdam University Press).

Ross, Kristin, Fast Cars and Clean Bodies: Decolonization and the Reordering of French Culture (Cambridge, Massachusetts: MIT Press, 1996).

Siclier, Jacques and Fabien Levy, Jules Dassin (Paris: Edilig, 1986).

Sorlin, Pierre, 'What Made a Popular Film in France in the 1950s', in B. Rigby and N. Hewitt (eds) France and the Mass Media (London: Macmillan, 1991) pp 68–84.

Tonnere, Jérôme, 'Peurs de la ville', Cinématographe, 63 (1980) pp. 3–10.

Vincendeau, Ginette, 'France 1945–1965 and Hollywood: the policier as international text', Screen, 33, no. 1 (1992) pp. 50–79.

Vincendeau, Ginette, 'Noir is Also a French Word: The French Antecedents of Film Noir', in I. Cameron (ed.) The Book of Film Noir (New York: Continuum, 1993) pp. 49–58.

Vincendeau, Ginette, 'Autistic Masculinity in Jean-Pierre Melville's Crime Thrillers', in A. Hughes and J. Williams (eds) *Gender and French Cinema* (Oxford: Berg, 2001) pp. 139–56.

Vincendeau, Ginette, *Jean-Pierre Melville 'An American in Paris'* (London: British Film Institute, 2003).

Vincendeau, Ginette, 'French Film Noir in the Classical Era', in A. Spicer (ed.) *European Film Noir* (Manchester: Manchester University Press, 2007) pp. 23–54.

Wall, Irwin M., *The United States and the Making of Postwar France, 1945–1954* (Cambridge: Cambridge University Press, 1991).

# Index